Food For Thought

25 Ways to Protect Yourself from Disease and Promote Excellent Health

Principles I Have Lived By

Ray Morgan, OM.D. Ph.D.

authorHOUSE®

AuthorHouse™
1663 Liberty Drive
Bloomington, IN 47403
www.authorhouse.com
Phone: 1-800-839-8640

First published by AuthorHouse   3/22/2011

ISBN: 978-1-4567-4808-1 (e)
ISBN: 978-1-4567-4809-8 (dj)
ISBN: 978-1-4567-4810-4 (sc)

Library of Congress Control Number: 2011903867

Printed in the United States of America

Unless otherwise indicated, Scriptures are taken from the Authorized (King James) version of the Holy Bible.
Book cover designed by Kwame Boyce
Copyedited by Janice I. Dixon
Proofreading by Felicia Underwood

A Message from My Lawyer:

This book is published under the first amendment of the United States Constitution, which grants the right to discuss openly, and freely all matters of public concern and to express viewpoints no matter how controversial or unaccepted they may be. Medical groups and pharmaceutical companies, however, have finally infiltrated and violated our sacred constitution. Therefore we are forced to give you the following WARNINGS.

This book is intended as an educational reference guide only, not a medical manual. The information given here is designed to help you make informed decisions about your health. It is not intended as a substitute for any treatment that may have been prescribed by your medical professional. The author takes no responsibility for the misinterpretation and deliberate or accidental misuse of the information presented in this book.

Therefore, if you are ill or have been diagnosed with any disease, please consult a competent medical doctor before attempting any natural healing program. Remember any one of the programs in this book could be potentially dangerous, even lethal. So if you must proceed, do so with CAUTION.

Foreword

In the 25+ years that I have known Dr. Ray (Imhotep) Morgan, I have seen the results of his work, and I have witnessed his passion for the healing of people who were (and are) in the trap of iatrogenic medicine. I have seen those who suffered with "incurable diseases" experience a second chance and become renewed, healthy individuals. Dr. Ray (Imhotep) Morgan has incarnated the spirit of Imhotep, the Father of Medicine, and this is why I gave him that designation at the Shrine of Imhotep in the Temple of Sobek, at Kom Ombo, Egypt in 2008!

As did the Grandmaster Builder and Great Physician, Imhotep, so does Dr. Ray (Imhotep) Morgan have a mandate from God to "HEAL THE SICK!" And as you read this book and apply the suggested remedies in it, you will see that the most outstanding quality that makes Dr. Morgan's approach to good health so effective is simplicity! The information that he gives and the remedies that he provides for the dis-eases that plague the lives of the people in our communities are inexpensive, painless, natural and easy to accomplish.

Although Dr. Morgan is a Doctor of Science, as a Doctor of Naturopathy (N.D.), he emphasizes a system of medicine that is based on the healing power of nature. His approach is, and has been, to find the cause of dis-ease by understanding the body, mind, and spirit of his clients. Then he utilizes a variety of therapies and techniques (i.e., nutrition, herbal medicine, homeopathy, applied kinesiology, iridology, acupuncture, as well as other ancient treatments and remedies) and achieves healings and success in his clients that he is world renown for.

In his practice, Dr. Morgan spends a great deal of time enhancing the body's own healing abilities of his clients. But for the many thousands who can't get to his office, he has provided this book to help empower them to make the necessary lifestyle changes that will provide the best possible course to good health. Not only will this book provide the knowledge necessary for the reader to appropriate a lifestyle to enhance their health, but it will also be a good resource for maintaining optimum health by helping the reader to take the appropriate steps to prevent dis-ease and educate others.

We live in a world where no one is free from the destructive elements in our environment that are constantly attacking our bodies and immune system, so everyone is literally suffering from dis-ease! Therefore, it is imperative that you learn the information in this book ...and then LIVE BY IT!

Always remember that the most important thing in life is having and maintaining good health. Some would disagree and say that the most important thing in life is spirituality and knowing the things of God. But the truth of the matter is that it is impossible to be at your spiritual best if you are not at your physical best! In fact, being in good health is the key to success in virtually every walk of life.

You may ask, "What is good health?" Simply stated, the answer to this question is, good health is when your body is free from mental and physical dis-ease(s). When your body is free from mental and physical dis-ease, you can acquire wealth, you can build a stronger family unit, you can spend better quality time with your grandchildren and loved ones, you can contribute more to those things that are important to you. You can do so much more when you are in good health!

Dr. Ray (Imhotep) Morgan is not only my friend and a colleague...he is also my physician as well! And because of his work in my life, I am better and much more effective at what I do. It is an honor to be a living testament to his work, his mission, and his purpose.

Ray Hagins, Ph.D.

Acknowledgement

To our son, Scott: When you were ten, I asked you to help me to be a better father because I had limited experience. You not only made me a better father, you made me a better man. You were taken from us much too soon. We will always love you. You are still giving us Hope...Time... Love...and Healing.

Tomorrow will come. The pain will ease. But you will always be alive and loved in our hearts.

To my sister, Rashida, and my mother-in- law, Queen Mother Marie Conway, and all my ancestors who have made their transition. It takes hope, time and love for the healing to take place. We will always accept, but never forget, though we might move on, we will never forget you or stop loving you. You are our heavenly angel and we love you so much, and miss you everyday!

And to all of us five billion human beings on earth who, by living love, can make our planet a here and now paradise.

I extend my special thanks to my publisher, to my editor, Janice I. Dixon, and proofreader, Felicia Underwood, for their professional guidance, patience and encouragement along another literary journey.

To my children Kristal, Nekia, and Tobias, my daughters-in-law Vixen and Hope; and my four grandchildren - Sakai, Kimari, Sanje and Adonis, I love you. You have provided the foundation for this work. Remember to keep your dreams alive, and to achieve anything in life requires faith, vision, hard work, determination, dedication and belief in yourself. All things are possible for those who believe.

Ray Morgan, OM.D. Ph.D.

Last, but not least, I would like to thank my wife Regina (Ankhesenamen) for her understanding and love during the past few years. Her support and encouragement was in the end what made this book possible.

~~***~~

Preface

"The doctor of the future will give no medicine, but will interest his patient in the care of the human frame, in diet and in the cause and prevention of disease." -Thomas Edison

This book will show you how to improve your health through a positive mental attitude, healthy lifestyle and health-promoting diet and supplements. It is stacked with practical tips and insights on disease prevention by enhancing key body systems. The bulk of the book details natural remedies for treating more than 70 ailments. Each includes symptoms, descriptions, therapeutic considerations (with discussion of studies), and a treatment summary, including nutritional supplements and botanical (herbal) medicines. If you have a disease, this book will give you a valuable perspective on natural treatments. If you're well, it will give you advice for maintaining and enhancing your health.

This little book will have a large impact on your life! Its offers simple and thought provoking truths for anyone at any age making an elementary change in their health. It will help you transform your life for the better in many aspects, teaching you straightforward lessons that will be useful for an entire lifetime.

Rooted in traditional Toltec beliefs, these four agreements are essential steps on the path to personal freedom: 1) Be impeccable with your word; Say only what you mean; The word is the most powerful tool humans have; 2) Don't take anything personally; Self-importance leads people to think they are the center of the universe, causing pain and injustice; 3) Don't make assumptions. To avoid frustration and blame, ask what is meant; 4) Always do your best. This is the surest way to avoid self-condemnation, though it is important to realize one's best is always changing.

Fresh Vegetable & Fruit Juices–What's Missing in Your Body?

By Norman W. Walker, D.Sc.

Dr. Olarsch considers this mandatory reading if you are using a juicer and excellent reading on health in general. If you want to learn the healing properties of each fruit and vegetable, and what to increase in your diet for specific health conditions, this book will not let you down! The deficiency of certain minerals, salts and vitamins can cause symptoms of illness. In this book, vegetable juices are listed according to categories and an explanation is provided of their elements. In cooperation with R. D. Pope, M.D., a formula guide is provided with suggestions for treating specific ailments.

"The only thing to do with good advice is pass it on. It is never any use to one self."

- Oscar Wilde

~~***~~

Table of Contents

Introduction:

Many years ago, I learned that before giving advice to anyone, I should first make sure that the person I am advising is actually soliciting my advice. He or she may just want me to listen to them and be a good friend, seeking only understanding, empathy, and compassion. I never assume that everyone wants my advice. I may have some insight into their problem, but I really need to listen attentively to their problems first for a very long time to understand the situation. If, and only if, my friend actually asks for my advice should I provide it.

It is a great honor to be asked for advice, but it is also a big responsibility. Good advice can help people make sound decisions or find the right path in life, while bad advice can have disastrous consequences. Fortunately, with a little forethought you can weed out good advice from the bad.

For the past fifteen years I've displayed on my desk a poster enumerating the twenty necessary principles to vibrant health that I have lived by. Over the years, many of my clients have asked me for copies of the poster and others suggested that I put these principles into a book. This is it: my twenty necessary principles for vibrant health, plus five additional principles.

Do you have a recurring ailment that does not seem to improve with treatments provided by traditional western medicine? If your answer is yes, then you're not alone. According to the National Center for Complementary and Alternative Medicine at the National Institutes of Health, thirty-six percent of U.S. adults have used at least one alternative or complementary treatment for an illness or chronic condition. Dangerous side effects from prescription drugs, experience with a misdiagnosis, botched surgery, or dealing with dismissive doctors are just some of the reasons many people decide to pursue alternative treatments. The use of alternative medicine, however, is not just merely the latest trend. These methods have been used for centuries to successfully treat people all around the world. There are so many alternative therapies to choose from, the problem then becomes how do you know which method might be right for you.

This book is an introduction to some of the most popular alternative and complementary therapies offered in the international natural health community today. The following twenty-five natural therapies that lead to vibrant health include: fresh juice, raw foods, vegan foods, colon cleansing and colonic irrigation, food combining, alkaline food, kidney and liver cleansing, walking and breathing, loving life, loving self, more sex, helping others, learning to relax, forgiveness, listening to your inner voice, and overall nutrition. Internal cleansing is an integral part of my own health regime. Each chapter provides a detailed, yet easy-to-understand overview of the therapy, including a brief history, its benefits, and what to expect from the therapy.

There Is a Threat Hanging Over Our Heads

Most Americans are not aware of a very powerful threat hanging over our heads. It's not terrorism, oil shortages, the economy, or some other political issue. The clearest and most pressing danger lies in the fact that every second an American is stricken with at least one chronic illness. (A chronic illness is an illness that must be constantly managed such as diabetes or hypertension.) As of the year 2000, the U.S. population was two hundred seventy-six million. Nearly half of the population — one hundred twenty five million Americans — lived with some type of chronic condition, and today sixty million have multiple chronic illnesses. More than three million — two million women and seven hundred fifty thousand men — live with five such conditions. There is no doubt that sickness affects us directly, causing untold suffering and hardship. I'm writing this book to help you to take back the responsibility for your own health.

So Why Are We Sick?

I'll be brutally honest here so there are no misunderstandings: We get sick because our lack of health is economically profitable for a lot of big companies and their shareholders. This includes:

- The food industry with all the 'designer' junk foods and

beverages that hold no nutritional value and actually make us fat and sick.

- All the polluting industries that fill our lives and bodies with harmful chemicals and toxins.

- The "sick care" industry that figured out long ago that there is a lot more money to be made in treating symptoms with drugs and surgeries in expensive hospitals than in patient education, prevention, and natural medicine.

Keeping American's sick is big business and very profitable. As professor Paul Zane Pilzer explains in his best-selling book, *The Wellness Revolution*: "Incredibly powerful economic forces are preventing people from taking control of their health and actually encouraging them to gain weight – forces so powerful that nothing short of a revolution will be able to stop them." From birth we've been bombarded with millions of commercials that turn us into happily paying consumers of the very things that make us sick. Now the only way for us to become and stay healthy for life is to train ourselves to see through all the commercial deception and brainwashing, and learn how to be healthy. This book provides insight into some natural things you can do for yourself.

~ ~***~ ~

Chapter One: Water — The Key to Life

The human body is composed of eighty-five percent water; it is so essential to our being. Our very life, as with all animal and plant life on our planet, is dependent upon water. We not only need water to grow our food, generate our power and run our industries, but we need it as a basic part of our daily lives — our bodies need it to ingest and absorb vitamins, minerals, amino acids, etc. It also detoxifies the liver, kidneys, and the other organs and carries waste from our cells. Our communities cannot exist without water. We can do without the comfort of shelter, even of food for a period, but we cannot be deprived of water and survive for more than a few days. Due this intimate relationship between water and life, water is woven into the fabric of all cultures, religions and societies in myriad ways.

Are You Dying of Thirst?

Well, you just might. It sounds so simple. H20. Two parts hydrogen, one part oxygen. But this substance, better known as water, is the most essential element, next to air, to our survival. Water truly is everywhere; still most take it for granted.

Water makes up more than two-thirds of the weight of the human body, and without it, we would die in a few days. The human brain is made up of 95% water, blood is 82% water, and lungs are 90% water. A mere 2% drop in our body's water supply can trigger signs of dehydration: fuzzy short-term memory, trouble with basic math computation, difficulty focusing on small print, such as on a computer screen. Are you having trouble reading this? Drink up! Mild dehydration is also one of the most common causes of daytime fatigue. An estimated seventy-five percent of Americans have mild, chronic dehydration. That's a pretty scary statistic for a developed country where water is readily available through the tap or a bottle.

Water is important to the mechanics of the human body. The body cannot work without it, just as a car cannot run without gas and oil. In fact, all the cell and organ functions in our entire anatomy and physiology depend on water for their functioning.

- Water serves as a lubricant.
- Water forms the base for saliva.
- Water forms the fluids that surround the joints.
- Water regulates body temperature through perspiration.
- Water helps to alleviate constipation by moving food through the intestinal tract; it's the best detoxification agent.
- Water regulates metabolism
- Water helps to digest our food and helps the body to absorb nutrients.
- Water is needed to detoxify the kidneys and the liver.
- Water is needed to carry away body waste.
- Water is necessary for fiber to do its work.

In addition to the daily maintenance of our bodies, water also plays a key role in the prevention of disease. Drinking eight glasses of water daily can decrease the risk of colon cancer by 45%, bladder cancer by 50% and can even potentially reduce the risk of breast cancer. And those are just a few examples. Since water is such an important component to our physiology, it would make sense that the quality of the water should be just as important as the quantity. Drinking water should always be clean and free of contaminants to ensure proper health and wellness.

According to recent news and reports, most tap and well water in the U.S. is not safe for drinking due to heavy industrial and environmental pollution. Toxic bacteria, chemicals, and heavy metals routinely penetrate and pollute our natural water sources making people sick while exposing them to long -term health consequences such as liver damage, cancer, and other serious conditions. We have reached the point where all sources of our drinking water, including municipal water systems, wells, lakes, rivers, and even glaciers contain some level of contamination. Even some brands of bottled water have been found to contain high levels of contaminants in addition to plastics chemicals leaching from the bottle.

A good water filtration system installed in your home is the only way to proactively monitor and ensure the quality and safety of your drinking water. Reverse osmosis water purification systems can remove 90-99 percent of all contaminants from city and well water to deliver healthy drinking water for you and your family.

Americans, as do many other fortunate people, take water availability for granted. The quantity of water used for household and other basic needs represents a relatively small amount of the total quantities relegated to other uses. We use five times the amount of water that Europeans use. Our daily use of water is approximately 190 liters (50 gallons) of water. We pay twenty-five cents for water use on a daily basis. Two-thirds of the water used in a home is used in the bathroom. Flushing a toilet requires 7.5 to 26.5 liters (2 to 7 gallons) of water. Showering for five-minutes requires 95 to 190 liters (25 to 50 gallons) of water. Brushing your teeth utilizes 7.5 (2 gallons) of water. For our automatic dishwasher 35 to 45 liters (9 to 12 gallons) of water is used.

Yet, water remains the most precious and highly sought commodity for billions of people. Despite the technological advances attained at this point in the twenty-first century, we have not mustered the skills, the resources, or the will to provide all members of the global population with something as basic as a safe water supply and adequate sanitation.

Humans need to drink, or ingest through food approximately five liters of water per person per day. This intake of water is most effective if taken during these times: two glasses after waking up to help activate internal organs; one glass thirty minutes before meals to aid digestion; one glass before taking a bath to help lower blood pressure; and one glass before going to bed to avoid strokes or heart attacks.

It is equally important to drink sufficient quantities of water throughout the day to insure your health and manage your weight. Drink at least three to four additional large (12 oz.) glasses a day. This can be in the form of filtered tap water, filtered bottled water, carbonated, flavored or mineral water, but don't drink mineral water exclusively because it could cause other problems. Try to avoid sweetened water. Also be sure to drink water before and after you play or workout. Carry a bottle of water with you while you're out-and-about shopping or walking.

We also need water to maintain a certain standard of personal and domestic hygiene sufficient to maintain good health. It is not sufficient merely to have access to water in adequate quantities, the water also needs to be of a good quality to maintain health and must be free of harmful biological and chemical pathogens. Water in many of the developing or third world countries often does not meet these criteria and places the users at risk. This is because one of the primary causes of contamination of water is the inadequate or improper disposal of human (and animal) waste. This often leads to a cycle of infection (resulting primarily in diarrhea diseases) and contamination, which remains one of the leading causes of illness and death in the developing world. Untreated water is drinking water that has not been treated, filtered, or boiled to eliminate infectious bacteria, viruses, and parasites (such as *Giardia lamblia and Escherichia coli, commonly known as E coli*). These organisms can cause diarrhea, illness and sometimes death. Many infections that result from drinking untreated water go away by themselves after a few days, but some require treatment. Giardiasis (also called giardia) is an illness caused by infection with the parasite *Giardia lamblia* (also known as *Giardia intestinalis). Giardiasis* is usually caused by drinking water that is contaminated with the parasite. In the United States, *G. lamblia* is most often found in untreated streams, rivers, and lakes. Symptoms of giardiasis include diarrhea, a lot of gas (flatulence), abdominal cramps, and nausea. In some people, giardiasis does not cause any symptoms. In other people, the symptoms may keep recurring. Infection with the parasite can be prevented by hand-washing and by treating water taken from rivers, lakes, or streams before drinking it or using it to cook, wash dishes, or brush teeth. Symptoms of giardiasis may go away on their own. But medicine, usually metronidazole, can relieve the discomfort and prevent the spread of the illness. Chlorination is the most widely used method of killing bacteria in water, but it is also known to produce powerful carcinogen residues, including dioxin. Studies have shown that the risk of bladder cancer is doubled if we drink chlorine-treated water. Chlorination also destroys Vitamin E in the body, which can lead to heart problems and has been linked to clogged arteries.

Distilled water may be the cleanest water available. It happens to be the best for cleaning and detoxifying the body. This is simply because distilled water is empty water (100 percent H2O) with no minerals to occupy space, so it dissolves and attracts impurities out of the body. It also happens to be the best water to use for making herbal tea because it will dissolve and accept more of the phytochemicals from the plant and therefore makes a stronger herbal tea. I also recommend Reverse Osmosis water as a near equivalent to distilled water.

Water and Weight Loss

Water is a great appetite suppressor. Have a glass one-half hour before every meal and snack. You'll fill up your stomach and naturally eat less. It is essential for weight loss and even more essential for keeping the weight off. Water metabolizes the fat that is stored in the body.

Studies have determined that when we drink enough water, less fat will stay in the body. If we decrease our water intake, however, more fat will be deposited in our body. This occurs because when the kidneys are not supplied with enough water, they cannot function properly and cannot handle all the fat.

Whatever fat the kidneys cannot handle is carried to the next "waste station" which is the liver. The liver's job is to metabolize the fat and turn it into energy the body can use. Any fat the liver cannot handle will be deposited in the body. So, you can see why drinking water is so important.

A study determined that women who drank five or more glasses of water a day had a 41% less risk of getting a heart attack than women that drank two or fewer glasses of water daily.

Here are some additional benefits to look forward to if you supply your body with plenty of water:

- You will have more energy.

- Your mental and physical performance will improve.

- Your skin will look and be healthier.

- It will be easier to lose weight.

- You'll have fewer headaches and/or dizzy spells.

Other natural remedies might be great. But they might even work better if we drank enough water.

~~***~~

Chapter Two:
Let Your Juicer Be Your Drug Store

Fresh juice is the most powerful natural blood builder and blood transfusion available. My clients often come to me anemic due to blood loss from injury, or an unsuccessful surgery, or disease such as cancer or leukemia. My job is to build their blood back up fast by replenishing lacking nutrients, iron, hemoglobin, etc. to keep them alive. Fresh juice is always the first in their itinerary. Fresh juice always works, bringing all blood levels back to normal within forty-eight hours, and it works 100% of the time.

Vegetable juicing is critical to good health because it is an important source of raw food. Each of us needs raw foods every day, and juicing is an excellent way to make certain you receive large quantities. Fruit juicing is certainly good for you, but it has one disadvantage over vegetable juicing: fruit juice tends to increase insulin levels when consumed. So be careful using fruit juice if you are a diabetic, hypo or hyperglycemic.

Vegetable juice will not raise your insulin levels like fruit juice. Carrot and beet juice are the only exceptions; both function like fruit. Nevertheless, fruit juicing is certainly better for you and your children than drinking soda, which is a very bad idea.

The concentrated amount of vitamins, minerals, enzymes, and other life-giving nutrients in juice assimilates in your mouth and into your cells, literally traveling to every organ and cell of your body in seconds. I have personally revived and brought dying patients back to life with a few gallons of fresh juice.

Why should I juice vegetables rather than eat them whole?

Many of us have relatively compromised intestines as a result of poor food choices over many years. A compromised intestine limits the ability of the body to absorb all the nutrients found in raw vegetables and fruits, but juicing tends to facilitate the absorption of many nutrients. Vegetable and fruit juicing is also well suited for the fast moving Western lifestyle. It makes it possible for busy people to add more healing foods into their diets with minimal effort. If I were to give you five carrots, a beet, and a bunch of celery to eat raw, I doubt you could eat all of them in one sitting. Drinking the vegetables in juice form would be far easier.

Can I make my vegetable juice in the morning and drink it later in the day?

Although this is much better than not drinking vegetable juice at all, it is best when it is freshly made. Vegetable juice is one of the most perishable foods there is and should all be consumed immediately. If you are careful, however, you can store your vegetable juice for up to twenty-four hours with only a moderate nutritional decline.

You can safely store vegetable juice by putting it in a glass jar, filling it to the very top, and sealing it with an airtight lid. The jar should be airtight because oxygen in the air will damage the juice and oxidized juice is undrinkable. Think of a cut apple turning brown when exposed to air.

It's a good idea to use an opaque container to block out all light, which also damages the juice, and then store it in the refrigerator until about thirty minutes prior to drinking. Ideally the juice should be consumed at room temperature.

Fresh juice naturally detoxifies your body by stimulating many elimination organs, i.e., your liver, gall bladder, kidneys, and intestines to eliminate more waste. It also cleanses, detoxifies, and heals these organs.

Fresh fruit and vegetable juice is naturally very alkalizing, i.e., cleansing and detoxifying to your blood. It facilitates the *phagocytosis*, or the speed and ability of your white blood cells, like macrophages, to clean your blood and tissues of bacteria, virus, fungus, and many harmful pathogenic microorganisms, even malignant cancer cells.

What type of vegetables should I juice?

Celery, fennel, cucumbers, and ginger are a good combination that is easily tolerated by those just starting out with juicing.

Unfortunately, these are not as beneficial as the more intense dark green vegetables. Once you get used to this tasty blend, you can start adding the more beneficial, but perhaps less palatable ones.

Green, leafy vegetables are the best to use in your vegetable juicing program. All varieties of lettuce are easy to use, including, but not restricted to:

Red leaf lettuce

Green Leaf lettuce

Romaine lettuce

Escarole lettuce

You can then add in other similar green leafy vegetables such as spinach, kale, and cabbage. Cabbage juice is one of the most healing juices when it comes to repairing ulcers, as it is a huge source of vitamin U. Vitamin U is found in raw cabbage and is thought to help with the healing of skin ulcers and ulcers in the digestive tract. The appropriate dosage is approximately one glass per day. Toxicity has not been determined; however, no one that I know of has ever had any side effects.

Herbs also make wonderful combinations. Parsley and cilantro are great in vegetable juice. (My favorite source is the one-pound bag with organic cilantro mixed with other herbs.)

One important note about the TASTE of vegetable juice

One major objection people raise when talking about vegetable juicing is the taste. "I can't stand it," they say. I tried to get a sick friend to drink one of my green juice recipes. He told me he drank the juice but I didn't see any positive results, so I had to get creative. I instructed him to add a few seedless grapes to the mixture and he loved the juice. The results were evident in his improved health. I highly recommend your using a few grapes if you find your vegetable juice unpalatable. It's a fantastic way to improve the taste. Adding two to three apples or a few kiwis also works well.

You must rotate the vegetables you are using in your vegetable juicing program

What is the best type of juice to use in my juicing program? Variety is not only the spice of life; it makes for better health. Try to rotate the kind of vegetables and fruits from one week to another in order to prevent allergic reaction to one or more of the fruits or vegetables.

Here are some juicing recipes that can remedy specific ailments. A standard serving size is eight ounces. Remember to wash all fruits and vegetables very well.

Alkaline Drink Juice Recipe

- Orange-Grapefruit-Lemon Juice: 1 orange, ¼ grapefruit, and ¼ lemon with skin. Remember to always discard the peel from the grapefruit and orange, leaving as much of the white under peel on them as possible.

- Carrot-Cabbage-Celery Juice: 3 carrots, 1 2-inch piece of cabbage, 1 stalk of celery

Natural Laxative Juice Recipe

- Apple-Pear Juice: 2 Granny Smith apples, 1 pear

Blood Purifier Recipe

- Apple-Strawberry Juice: 3 Golden Delicious or other sweet apples, 8 strawberries

Anti-Virus/Cold Prevention - high in vitamin C

- Apple-Kiwi Juice: 2 apples, 4 kiwis

- Apple-Orange Juice: 2 apples, 1 orange (peel and discard skin of the orange)

- Pineapple-Tangerine Juice: 1 1-inch thick pineapple round, 3-4 tangerines (peel and discard skin of tangerine)

Immune System Support – high in vitamin A

- Carrot-Celery-Apple-Beet-Wheatgrass-Parsley Juice: 3 carrots, 1 stalk celery, 1 apple, ½ beet with greens, ½ handful wheatgrass, and ½ handful parsley (you can substitute 1 whole handful of parsley if wheatgrass is unavailable)

Blood Regenerator (high in iron and chlorophyll) –

- Carrot-Spinach-Lettuce-Turnip-Parsley Juice: 5 carrots, 6 spinach leaves, 4 lettuce leaves, ¼ turnip, and 4 sprigs of parsley

Internal Body Cleanser Juicing Recipe

- Carrot-Cucumber-Beet Juice: 2-3 carrots, ½ cucumber, and ½ beet with greens. You can substitute ½ zucchini for the cucumber

Bone Building Tonic – high in calcium

- Carrot-Kale-Parsley-Apple Juice: 5-6 carrots, 4 kale leaves, and 4 sprigs of parsley, ½ apple

Lung Tonic Juicing Recipe

- Carrot-Parsley-Potato-Watercress Juice: 5 carrots, 4 sprigs parsley, ¼ potato, and 4 sprigs watercress

What is the best juicer?

There are several juicers available by just as many manufacturers. In my opinion, however, the three best are the Vita Mix, the Health Master and the Norwalk juicers. Many of what we call juicers really are not *juicers* but *extractors*. Popular brands of juice extractors include Juice Man, Jack LaLane, the Omega, the Breville, and Samson. Extractors separate the pulp from the juice, but juicers mix the entire vegetable or fruit leaving both pulp and juice together for a more synergetic balance.

Cleaning your juicer is important

It's important to clean your juicer immediately after each use to prevent contamination from mold growth. I regularly clean my juicer by dropping in a few pieces of garlic, running the juicer for a minute, and then rinsing it thoroughly.

Before drinking your freshly prepared juice, it is important to add some of its missing ingredients such as fish oil, flaxseed oil, evening primrose oil, and cod liver oil (a source of omega 3 fatty acids, vitamin D and A, in addition to the EPA/DHA.) Because vegetable juice has virtually no fat and the manifestation of fat depends on the vegetables' use, most likely there will be no protein present in your juice. Therefore, it would be a good idea to balance your drink by adding the recommended essential oils and some protein supplement.

~~***~~

Chapter Three:
Eat More Live, Raw Food

The majority of enzymes in raw foods are destroyed by heat

Live food equals life. Living food is filled with enzymes, vitamins, and hundreds of other nutritional substances that are destroyed by heating, cooking, and processing of food. Eating food raw and sprouted gives you a nutritional blast that is second only to juices. Eating live food brings life back into your body.

Like our bodies, most raw foods are perishable. When raw foods are exposed to temperatures above 118 degrees, they rapidly start to break down, just as our bodies would with a high fever. One of the constituents of foods, which can break down, is enzymes. Enzymes help us digest our food. Enzymes are proteins though, and they have a very specific three-dimensional structure in space. Once they are heated much above 118 degrees, this structure can change.

Once enzymes are exposed to heat, they are no longer able to provide the function for which they were designed. Cooked foods contribute to chronic illness because their enzyme content is damaged, thus the body must make its own enzymes. Valuable metabolic enzymes are used, and the digestion of cooked food demands much more energy than the digestion of raw food. In general, raw food is so much more easily digested that it passes through the digestive tract in one-half to one-third of the time it takes for food that is cooked.

Eating enzyme-depleted foods places a burden on our pancreas and other organs and overworks them, which eventually exhausts these organs. Many people gradually impair their pancreas and progressively lose the ability to digest their food after a lifetime of ingesting processed foods, leading to many of our diseases.

The Effect of Raw Food versus Cooked Food

In 1930, under the direction of Dr. Paul Kouchakoff, research was conducted at the Institute of Clinical Chemistry in Lausanne, Switzerland. The effect on the immune system of cooked and processed versus raw and natural foods was tested and documented, and the research revealed important discoveries concerning leukocytes, i.e., white blood cells.

The researchers observed that after a person eats cooked food, his/her blood responds immediately by increasing the number of white blood cells. This is a well-known phenomenon called *digestive leukocytosis*, in which there is a rise in the number of leukocytes after eating. Since digestive leukocytosis always was observed after a meal, it was considered to be a normal physiological response to eating. No one knew why the number of white cells rose after eating, since this appeared to be a stress response, as if the body was somehow reacting to something harmful such as infection, exposure to toxic chemicals, or trauma.

The Swiss researchers, however, made a remarkable discovery. They found that eating raw, unaltered food did not cause a reaction in the blood. In addition, they found that if a food had been heated beyond a certain temperature (unique to each food), or if the food was processed (refined, chemicals added, etc.), this always caused a rise in the number of white cells in the blood.

The researchers renamed this reaction *pathological leukocytosis*, since the body was reacting to highly altered food. They tested many different types of foods and found that if the foods were not refined or overheated, they caused no reaction. The body saw them as "friendly foods." If heated at too high a temperature, however, these same foods caused a negative reaction in the blood found only when the body is invaded by a dangerous pathogen or trauma.

The worst offenders of all, whether heated or not, were processed foods which had been refined (such as white flour and white rice), or pasteurized (a process in which milk is flash-heated to high temperatures to kill bacteria), or homogenized (also seen in milk where the fat in milk is subjected to artificial suspension), or preserved (chemicals are added to food to delay spoilage or to enhance texture or taste).

In other words, the offenders were foods that were changed from their original God-given state.

Raw foods and digestive enzymes

Let's get back to enzymes. Raw foods are rich in enzymes. Enzymes are needed for the digestive system to work. They are necessary to break down food particles so they can be utilized for energy. The human body makes approximately twenty-two different digestive enzymes that are capable of digesting carbohydrates, protein, and fats. Raw vegetables and raw fruit are rich sources of enzymes.

While all raw foods contain enzymes, the most powerful enzyme-rich foods are sprouted seeds, grains, and legumes. Sprouts are one of the most complete and nutritional of all foods that exist. Sprouts are rich with vitamins, minerals, proteins, and enzymes. Their nutritional value was discovered by the Chinese thousands of years ago. Over the past several years, numerous scientific studies in the U.S. have shown the importance of sprouts in a healthy diet.

Lack of digestive enzymes can be a factor in food allergies. Symptoms of digestive enzymes depletion are bloating, belching, gas, bowel disorders, abdominal cramping, heartburn, and food allergies.

One of my great teachers, the late Dr. Bernard Jenson, among many others, always promoted the eating of seeds when consuming grapes, apples, watermelons or almost any seed-bearing foods. This great doctor knew that the seeds contained the life. Isn't it interesting that today, many fruits are being grown seedless for eating convenience and not for nutrition?

Life energy, life force, enzymes, whatever you want to call it, is something that we seemed to have forgotten. Go ahead, dig a hole, plant a vitamin, or a mineral, or a hamburger, or a loaf of bread, or any cooked food for that matter, and see what happens. Nothing. You can water it, feed it, and pray, chant, or even sleep over it and I promise you absolutely nothing is going to happen, except that it is going to rot. If you plant a little sunflower seed, a massive explosion of life will blossom and grow twice as tall as you. Plant a raw almond and you will get a huge tree. For this reason alone, eating live, raw life-forced filled food is preferable. Life energy, enzymes and plant phytochemicals that create growth and life nourish your body in a much more powerful way than any cooked food.

~~***~~

Chapter Four:
Let It Be Vegan Food

The most powerful way to heal disease and detoxify and build your body is with *vegan* food. The vegan does not eat any animals or animal by-products.

The basis for vegan nutrition is derived from vegetarianism. But there are distinct differences between living a vegan lifestyle and living a vegetarian lifestyle. Unlike vegetarians, vegans are committed to living without products made or tested on animals and refuse to eat any meat, egg, or dairy foods. Vegan nutrition can be traced back as early as biblical times. Passages in the Bible discuss how certain religions believed in the overall preservation of health, the safety of animals, and the protection of one's environment. The term "vegan," came into use around 1944, when the Vegan Society was formed in the United Kingdom.

The Vegan Lifestyle

What does it mean to be a vegan? Upholding the philosophy of a vegan lifestyle involves making some critical changes in what you eat and what you buy. Vegans believe that using animals as a source for livestock, e.g., as a means to test new products, is cruel and inhumane. Therefore, instead of eating a vegetarian diet, which includes the consumption of dairy and egg products, vegans make the choice to go completely animal-free. How dedicated you are to the cause of veganism will depend on how far you go to eliminate animals from your lifestyle. Some vegans avoid using any leather products, eating honey, or buying cosmetics that have been tested on animals.

Documented benefits of a vegan lifestyle include permanent reduction in weight, blood pressure, serum cholesterol, and blood sugar, as well as reduced risk of cardiovascular disease and half dozen common forms of cancer. Allergies, arthritis, and asthma also respond to vegan nutrition. I also ask that you discontinue smoking, alcohol consumption, and that you begin or continue a graded exercise program.

Why Be a Vegan?

Well, why not? Approximately one and one-half million people in our country will die, this year alone, because the fat and cholesterol they consumed from eating animal products killed them. That is about two people every minute. It either physically clogged their heart's coronary arteries, giving them heart attack, or clogged the cerebral arteries to their brain, giving them a stroke, or clogged other important blood supply lines to other major organs, depriving them of oxygen and nutrients leading to degeneration and disease. Cholesterol increases blood viscosity and blood platelet sticking (clotting), which kills by causing high blood pressure and can lead to cancer. Heart disease, stroke, most cancer, even prostate disease (BPH) and fibroid uterine tumors are now linked to eating animals. Most diseases are now found to be literally "diseases of the fork." They are diseases caused by eating animals.

It is a well-known fact that meat is not good for our health. Yes, there is no longer any doubt about this fact.

The list of diseases known to be associated with meat looks like the index of a medical textbook. Anemia, appendicitis, arthritis, breast cancer, cancer of the colon, cancer of the prostate, constipation, diabetes, gall stones, gout, high blood pressure, indigestion, obesity, piles, strokes, and varicose veins are just some of the well known disorders which are more likely to affect meat eaters than vegetarians.

Avoiding meat is one of the best and simplest ways to cut down your fat consumption. Those who still eat beef are, in my view, foolishly exposing themselves to the risk of contracting the horrifying human version of Mad Cow Disease.

Add to those hazards the fact that if you eat meat you may be consuming hormones, drugs and other chemicals that have been fed to the animals before they were killed, and you can see the extent of the danger. No one knows precisely what effect eating the hormones in meat is likely to have on your health. But the risk is there and I think it's a big one. Some farmers use tranquillizers to keep animals calm. Others routinely use antibiotics so that their animals do not develop infections. When you eat meat you are, inevitably, eating those drugs. In America, over half of all animals are fed antibiotics, and I don't think it is any coincidence that the percentage of staphylococci infections resistant to penicillin went up from 13% in 1960 to 91% in 1988.

It is these synthetic hormones in meat that does the most harm, making meat-eating a greater health hazard than smoking. Simply avoiding red meat does not minimize the danger. If you want to eat a truly healthy diet then you must give up eating meat completely.

There are, of course, all sorts of old-fashioned myths about eating meat. At one time it was my belief that people who didn't eat meat would be short of protein, but that is now known to be absolute nonsense. It is equally untrue that if you don't eat meat your diet will be deficient in essential vitamins or minerals. Meat contains absolutely no more protein, vitamins, or minerals than your body cannot obtain from a vegetarian diet.

On the other hand, all the essential organic nutrients required in the human diet (essential amino acids, essential fatty acids, and vitamins) are made by plants and micro-organisms, not by animals. Animal foods contain those items too, but since most animals have roughly the same nutrient requirements as humans, we get the nutrients second-hand. The only ingredients unique to animal foods are cholesterol and saturated fat.

Vegan eating is very simple. One could consume only vegetables, grains, starches, and fruit, and still meet all one's Recommended Dietary Allowances (RDAs) for essential nutrients, except for vitamin B-12.

Vegan Nutrition and Weight Loss

A vegan diet is a weight loss fanatic's dream. A whole food vegan diet contains no refined sugar and no oil. The food recommendations are centered on fresh vegetables, particularly leafy greens, preferably raw, in whatever arrangement your taste buds appreciate the most, with calorie requirements filled in by starchy foods (potatoes, yams, etc.), grains (brown rice, pasta, etc.), and fresh fruit (to satisfy that ole sweet tooth).

No restriction is placed on the amount of this food you eat, and I encourage you to eat as much as you want as long as it's whole food (unrefined) and vegan. It is not necessary to measure or count servings or amounts consumed. Your body has three sensing mechanisms that take care of that automatically. First, your stomach, which has a one-quart capacity, has stretch receptors that send signals to the brain when the stomach is full. Second, your body will instruct you to eat until enough food energy is on board to run your metabolism, since calorie acquisition is arguably the main reason for eating. Third, complicated biochemical feedback systems detect the presence or absence of minerals, vitamins, essential fatty acids, and essential amino acids (protein).

Food Guide:

Base your diet on fresh vegetables, then fill in calorie requirements with fresh fruit, starches, and grains. Grains and starches are good foods, but when refined they release sugar rapidly, and raise insulin and triglyceride levels. These are foods you want to have as secondary.

"And God said, Behold, I have given you every herb bearing seed, which *is* upon the face of all the earth, and every tree, in the which *is* the fruit of a tree yielding seed; to you it shall be for meat." -Genesis.1:29

This biblical quote says nothing about dairy, eggs, fish, grain, meat, oil, poultry, or sugar. From the evolutionary standpoint the dietary advice comes out the same. Our remote primate ancestors evolved over fifty six million years living in trees where the food supply was mostly fruit, leaves, and nuts. Most of our physiology developed on these foods. Three million years ago our hominid ancestors descended to the ground and began adding meat to the diet as a survival strategy, but all the essential amino acids, fatty acids, and vitamins in the human diet are still synthesized by plants, not animals.

Milk was never a large part of the adult human diet until the agricultural revolution twelve thousand years ago. Oils were never part of the diet until fifty-five thousand years ago and that culinary disaster known as "frying" first appeared in the English language in1100 AD. Refined sugar did not enter the diet until four hundred years ago. From an evolutionary standpoint these are short time periods, and humans are poorly adapted to animal source food, vegetable oil, and refined sugar. Most of the degenerative diseases of our time are at least partly due to our departure from the diet on which we evolved.

The healthiness of a vegetarian diet is perhaps shown most dramatically by the fact that lifelong vegetarians visit hospitals 22% less often than meat eaters and for shorter stays. Vegetarians tend to be more fit and healthier than meat eaters, and many of the world's most successful athletes — particularly those who specialize in endurance events — follow a strictly vegetarian diet.

Becoming healthier isn't the only reason for turning green. Many who stop eating meat do so for moral and ethical reasons as much as for personal gain. Every minute of every working day thousands of animals are killed in slaughterhouses. Many animals are bled to death. Pain and misery are commonplace - for animals suffer from pain and fear just as much as you do.

In an average lifetime, the average meat eater will consume thirty-six pigs, thirty-six sheep and 750 chickens and turkeys. More and more people are deciding that they just don't want that much carnage on their consciences. It is never too late to stop eating meat.

In addition, more and more people are becoming aware of the fact that hunger around the world could be eradicated if rich westerners stopped eating meat. Every year over four-hundred million tons of grain is fed to livestock so that the world's rich can eat meat. Meanwhile, five hundred million people in poor countries are starving to death.

Many of those who toy with the idea of turning vegetarian because they want to be healthier, or to stop world starvation, or because they want to discourage the barbaric trade of breeding and killing animals for food, worry about what they are going to eat. Such worries are quite unnecessary.

There are not only many different fruits and vegetables available these days but, if you miss the texture of meat, you can buy vegetarian sausages, hamburgers, and pies. Stews and curries can be made with Soya and you can buy tofu cheese too.

To stay healthy, eat raw foods whenever possible (remember that cooking and reheating foods destroy vitamins and minerals) and use as little water as possible when boiling vegetables to avoid losing water soluble vitamins B and C. Steaming or stir frying vegetables is preferable to boiling.

Also try to eat fruit and vegetables in their skins because vitamins are often stored just below the skin. Be imaginative when shopping. You can get the iron, calcium, zinc, and other essential minerals that your body needs by eating dark green, leafy vegetables, nuts, pulses, sunflower seeds and dried fruits.

~~***~~

Chapter Five:
Cleanse Your Colon

From your mouth to your anus, your intestines are as long as two cars parked end to end. Since Americans have the highest incidence of colon disease and cancer in the world, knowing what goes on in the last five feet of your intestines can save your life.

Facts:

- In 2009, colon cancer killed 400% more people than AIDS. It actually kills more men and women in America than breast cancer or prostate cancer.

- 100% of Americans eventually have diverticulosis or many diverticula. Diverticula are the out-pouching of the wall of the colon, and are the result of a diet low in fiber. Up to 50% of Americans have polyps in their colon.

- Colon rectal cancer will kill about 60,000 Americans this year with approximately 130,000 new cases to be diagnosed.

- In my clinic, 80% of my clients' diseases were gone after completing a colon program.

Why a Clean Colon is Necessary

Bowel movements are the basis of your health. If you don't have at least two bowel movements per day, you are already walking your way toward disease. Our body has not changed very much in the past several thousand years but our diet has changed significantly. All the refined sugar, white flour, and meats filled with hormones and antibiotics we constantly ingest constitute an assault on our bodies. We are continuously violating our bodies by eating terrible foods, and colon cancer is the second leading cause of cancer deaths in America. Therefore, it is vitally important that all congestion and toxins be removed from the body, and it must begin with cleansing of the bowel.

One of the most frequent bowel problems that people experience today is constipation. A constipated system is one in which the transition time of toxic wastes is slow. The longer the "transit time," the longer the toxic waste matter sits in our bowel, which allows them to putrefy, ferment, and possibly be reabsorbed. The longer your body is exposed to putrefying food in your intestines, the greater the risk of developing disease. Even with one bowel movement per day, you will still have at least three meals worth of waste matter putrefying in your colon at all times.

Disease usually begins with a toxic bowel. Those having fewer bowel movements are harboring a potentially fertile breeding ground for serious diseases. Infrequent or poor quality bowel movements over an extended period of time may be very hazardous to your health.

Natural Colon Cleansing

More often than not, natural colon cleansing means following a special diet along with taking some colon-cleansing herbal supplements which are known to kill parasites and worms, contain digestive enzymes, provide probiotics (beneficial bacteria), and stimulate the liver, the gallbladder, and the intestines. Additional herbs may also include psyllium husk or seeds, Cascara Sagrada, flax seeds, slippery elm, and others.

The person on a typical American diet holds eight meals of undigested food and waste material in their colon, while the person on the high fiber diet holds only three. Try finding an herbal Colon Cleansing Program from your local herb shop that contains some of the above herbs and follow the program.

A proper colon-cleansing program removes mucoid plaque and parasites from the colon. Even a thin layer of mucoid plaque weakens the body. Nature intended mucoid plaque to be sloughed off. But due to stress and diet, most Americans have many hardened layers of mucoid plaque. The healthy colon weighs about four pounds. One autopsy revealed a colon choked with forty pounds of impacted mucoid plaque. A proper colon cleanse and detoxification program prepares your body for optimal health by removing the mucoid plaque.

It is always good to begin transitioning to a diet rich in raw fruits and vegetables with very few cooked or processed foods to help keep your digestive system free of mucoid plaque. Regular and easy elimination will be the rule, toxins will not build up and foods will be fully digested and utilized. This optimum nutrition allows rejuvenation and peak vitality. Of course it was a process of years or decades to get the body so full of plaque and toxins, so it will be a process, although faster, to detoxify and get your body pure and back to its highest possible state of health.

Colon cleansing is a procedure which may include the use of many different supplements, as listed above, along with a few days of fasting during the cleanse. A good intestinal cleanse will also include a parasite cleanse.

Colon Irrigation Hydrotherapy

Irrigation of the colon has been practiced in various forms by individuals and health care professionals for years, and has been beneficial to many health concerns. Enemas are the predecessors to modern day colonic irrigation.

In the early 1900's the mainstream medical community regularly utilized enemas in conjunction with their other health modalities. But now, colon hydrotherapy is practiced as an adjunctive therapy in complementary and alternative medicine or as a primary therapy by certified colon hydro therapists.

The common enema typically used by your grandparents and their parents has always been limited in its ability to treat and cleanse the lower bowel and the entire length of the colon. Enema water injected at an initial pressure of approximately two pounds per square inch and at very low volumes, cannot deliver its cleansing benefits past the sigmoid colon region. This leaves nearly 80% of the large intestine untreatable and serves only to soften stool in the region.

These cleansing limitations, however, are not present when one uses a modern colon hydrotherapy machine. The state-of-the-art colon hydrotherapy equipment in use therapeutically today cleanses the whole colon.

The advantages of colon hydrotherapy over the enema include:

- Dislodging entrapped fecal matter above the sigmoid colon area.
- Discharge of unfriendly bacteria and candida yeast.
- Promotion of essential and natural bacterial flora.
- Restoration of natural peristaltic muscle activity.
- Elimination of parasitic residences.

Enemas are simply unable to accomplish this range of therapeutic benefits. Additional medical treatments using laxatives, drug therapy, or surgery are generally not viable alternatives for the long-term restoration and promotion of colon health.

Modern advancements in colon hydrotherapy machines now enable the physician, colon hydrotherapist, or even private individuals using home therapy units to effectively treat common digestive problems, including constipation.

Modern colon hydrotherapy equipment allows individuals to overcome the shortcomings of traditional enema treatments in the comfort of their own homes.

Colonics cleanse the entire length of the colon. Enemas cleanse the lower part of the colon, the sigmoid, and part of the descending colon.

Colonics involve multiple infusions of water into the colon. Enemas involve a single infusion of water into the colon.

The advantages of these instruments are many:

1. Delivery systems and equipment can accurately measure and precisely deliver enough temperature-controlled water to be therapeutically effective throughout virtually the entire length of the colon.

2. Colon hydrotherapy equipment can sustain a regulated and safe injection pressure to permit cleaning water to reach the extremities of the colon. Water pressure under three psi gently

expands the folds of the colon wall to release entrapped fecal matter.

3. Multiple built-in safety features eliminate the possibility of over pressurizing the bowel and the sterilization of the unit. Modern colon hydrotherapy equipment is manufactured through compliance with strict FDA guidelines that dictate rigorous accountability. The FDA-registered equipment features temperature-controlled water mixing and back flow prevention valves, pressure and temperature sensors, and a built-in chemical sanitizing unit and/or water purification unit. Disposable single-use rectal tubes, and/or speculums are used. Always be sure to attend only International Association for Colon Hydrotherapy (I-act) certified colon-hydro therapists or clinics.

4. Cleansing water temperature is closely controlled with built-in safety features eliminating harmful temperature variations.

5. A self-administered, uniquely designed speculum is used to permit the pressure and temperature-controlled cleansing water to be introduced into the colon in a controlled manner and sanitarily flushed into existing medical office or home plumbing sewage systems.

Colon hydrotherapy can also be extremely helpful in restoring a healthy bacterial balance. When properly administered, colon hydrotherapy flushes out harmful bacteria from the large intestine.

Although healthy bacteria are also flushed out, the healthier colon environment greatly enhances the possibility for growth of friendly bacteria to restore and maintain a healthy bacterial balance.

The Benefits of a Colon Irrigation Session:

*   Working with a skilled therapist, a colonic can be an enlightening, educational experience.

*   You will expand your awareness of your body's functions including signals from your abdomen, skin, face, and eliminations.

- You will find that you can stop the beginnings of developing conditions through clues from these body regions and functions before they become serious. You can deal with them sooner and more easily than you otherwise might if you waited until they produced symptoms seen elsewhere in the body.

- It helps to alleviate constipation. The transverse colon passes through the solar plexus, which is the emotional center of the body. If an emotional event is left uncompleted, it often results in physical tension being stored there affecting all of the organs in that area, including the colon. This on going tightening of the colon muscle results in diminished movement of fecal materials through the colon, otherwise known as constipation.

- It will assist you in creating a fully holistic view of your body's functioning, which can lead to a better quality of life.

A Colon Irrigation Session Results In:

1. Removal of broken down toxic material so it can no longer harm your body or inhibit assimilation and elimination. Even debris built up over a long period of time is gently removed in the process of a series of treatments. Once impacted material is removed, your colon can begin to function again as it was intended. In a very real sense, a colonic is a rejuvenation treatment.

2. Exercise of the colon muscles. The build-up of toxic debris weakens the colon and impairs its functioning. The gentle filling and emptying of the colon improves peristaltic (muscular contraction) activity by which the colon naturally moves material.

3. Reshaping of the colon. When problem conditions exist in the colon, its shape is altered, which in turn causes more problems. The gentle action of the water, coupled with massage techniques from the colon therapist, helps to eliminate bulging pockets of waste and narrowed, spastic construction, enabling the colon to resume its natural shape.

4. Stimulation of reflex points. Every system and organ of the body is connected to the colon by reflex points. A colonic stimulates these points, thereby affecting the corresponding body parts in a beneficial way.

Parasites Removal Is Essential

The "Black Plague" ravaged Medieval Europe and killed twenty-five million people in just five years beginning in 1347. The "Plague" was caused by a single cell parasite called Yersinia pestis. You've heard the children's rhyme: "Ring around the rosy (sign of the plague on the skin) pocket full of posies (to hide the sent of death), ashes, ashes, (the corpses had to be burned) we all fall down (everyone died)." There are two forms of "Plague," the Bubonic Plague (death rate, 30-75%) and the Pneumonic Plague (death rate 90-95%). The Pneumonic Plague was spread to humans by the Oriental rat flea, took from one to seven days for plague signs to become visible, and resulted in death within twenty-four hours.

Today 85-95% of adults harbor parasites in their bodies but don't know it. You may be one of the unlucky ones. Parasites are a serious public health threat because so few people are talking about them, and even fewer people are listening.

Parasites are insidious because of the common misconception among medical professionals and the general public that parasites are a Third World problem where malnutrition and poor hygienic practices exist. Nothing could be farther from the truth. Tests often do not show the presence of parasites because the testing procedures are by and large outdated and inadequate.

An article in the *Miami Herald*, June 27, 1978, reported results of a nationwide survey conducted in 1976 by the Centers for Disease Control, which revealed that one in every six randomly selected people had one or more parasites.

Louis Parrish, M.D., a New York City physician specializing in parasites, wrote in 1991, in a web site article entitled "Parasites," "based upon my experience, I estimate in the New York metropolitan area that 25% percent of the population is infected ...Projections for the year 2025 suggest that more than half of the 8.3 billion people on Earth will then be infected with parasitic diseases."

"We have a tremendous parasite problem right here in the America, it's just not being identified." - Peter Weina, Ph.D., Chief of Pathobiology, Walter Reed Army Institute of Research, 1991

"I strongly believe that every patient with disorders of immune function, including multiple allergies (especially food allergy), and patients with unexplained fatigue or with chronic bowel symptoms should be evaluated for the presence of intestinal parasites." - Galland, Leo M.D. *Townsend Letter for Doctors*, 1988

"Make no mistake about it, worms are the most toxic agents in the human body. They are one of the primary underlying causes of disease and are the most basic cause of a compromised immune system." Parcells, Hazel D.C., N.D., Ph.D., 1974

Who Gets Parasites?

Everyone can potentially become a host to parasites. Let's look at some of the possible reasons for the rising number of parasitic infections:

- Return of armed forces from overseas.
- Continued popularity of household pets.
- Increasing popularity of exotic regional foods.
- Use of antibiotics and immunosuppressive drugs.
- The sexual revolution.

There are four pathways through which we can get infected:

- Via food or water which are sources of the roundworm, amoebae, giardia.
- Via a vector - the mosquito is a carrier of dog heartworm, filaria, malaria; the flea is a carrier of dog tapeworm; the common housefly transmits amebic cysts; the sand fly carries leishmaniasis.
- Via sexual contact where partners can transmit trichomonas, giardia, amoebae.
- Through the nose and skin where pinworm eggs and toxoplasma gondii can be inhaled from contaminated dust, hookworms, and schistosomes; strongyloides can penetrate exposed skin and bare feet.

Another parasitic pathway is the airplane. Extensive international travel has exposed people to a whole range of exotic diseases never before encountered in their homeland.

Why Doctors Often Don't Diagnose Parasites

Many parasite-based problems can mimic diseases, which are more familiar to most doctors. Roundworm infection has been mis-diagnosed as peptic ulcer. Amoebic colitis is often mis-labeled as ulcerative colitis. Chronic fatigue syndrome and yeast infections may be a chronic case of giardiasis. Diabetes and hypoglycemia may be caused by tapeworm infection.

Parasitology courses (the study of human parasites) are usually offered by a tropical disease department, which explains why the medical community generally perceives parasites as primarily a foreign concern. In addition, it is difficult to accurately diagnose the problem because the parasites' own reproductive cycle in which eggs or cysts are passed at irregular intervals makes diagnoses tricky.

These Are Some of The Symptoms of Parasite Infestation:

- Feel tired most of the time (chronic fatigue)?
- Have digestive problems (gas, bloating, constipation or diarrhea which come and go but never really clear up)?
- Have gastrointestinal symptoms and bulky stools with excess fat in feces?
- Suffer with food sensitivities and environmental intolerance?
- Developed allergic-like reaction and can't understand why?
- Have joint and muscle pains and inflammation often assumed to be arthritis?
- Suffer with anemia or iron deficiency (pernicious anemia)?
- Have hives, rashes, weeping eczema, cutaneous ulcers, swelling, sores, popular lesions, and itchy dermatitis?
- Experience anal itching?
- Suffer with restlessness and anxiety?

- Sinus problems?

- Abdominal, uterine or leg cramps?

- Always hungry?

- Experience multiple awakenings during the night?

- Grind your teeth?

- Have an excessive amount of bacterial or viral infections?

- Depressed?

- Difficulty gaining or losing weight no matter what you do?

- Did a Candida program, which either didn't help at all or helped somewhat but you still can't stay away from bread, alcohol, fruit, or fruit juices?

- Just can't figure out why you don't feel great and neither can your doctor? Perhaps you have eaten at a sushi bar, salad bar, or buffet?

Fast When You Cleanse

"Humans live on one-quarter of what they eat; and the other three-quarters lives by their doctor." – Imhoptep Egyptian pyramid inscription, 3800 B.C. The Father of Medicine

"Very few people know what real health is, because most are occupied with killing themselves slowly." - Albert Szent-Gyorgyi, Ph.D., Hungarian-born American biochemist; Nobel Prize in physiology and medical science

Before we look at how to fast, let's examine the question: "Why fast?" Although hundreds of fasting centers and clinics have existed in most European countries throughout the 20th century, Americans are still very far behind the learning curve regarding scientific, therapeutic fasting, as well as in adopting natural and organic food diets.

Imhotep of Egypt is believed to have been the author of the Edwin Smith Papyrus in which more than ninety anatomical terms and forty-eight injuries are described. He also may have founded a school of medicine in Memphis as a part of his cult center, possibly known as "Asklepion" which remained famous for two thousand years. All of this occurred some 2,200 years before the western Father of Medicine, Hippocrates, was born. Of Imhotep, Sir William Osler says he was the "first figure of a physician to stand out clearly from the mists of antiquity," having diagnosed and treated over 200 diseases.

Despite Imhotep having fasted and having prescribed fasting as ascribed on the walls of the Egyptian Pyramid in 3800 B.C., and Hippocrates, Galen and Paracelsus, declaring fasting "the greatest remedy, the physician within," the fact remains that symptoms-oriented, American- trained physicians are in the dark. In America, many in the medical orthodoxy continue to take a negative view of fasting, particularly as a therapeutic tool. But when the medical profession shifts gears from treating illness to PREVENTING illness, fasting will be increasingly prescribed.

How Should I Fast

I recommend juice fasting over water fasting, but I do not recommend fasting for more than three days without supervision by a competent medical professional, i.e., a physician. In preparation for your first day of fasting, you may want to take a few days to eliminate some foods or habits from your diet. Eliminating alcohol, nicotine, sugar, and caffeine from your diet will give you a more thorough clean with fewer side effects. It also is helpful to stop taking all nutritional supplements before beginning your fast.

Many people do well by preparing for their fasts with three to four days of consuming only fruits and vegetables. These foods nourish and slowly detoxify the body so that the actual fasting will be less intense.

How Do I Start My Fast

The first day of fasting (actually 24 hours, including the nights—7:00 a.m. until 7:00 a.m. the following day) gives you an opportunity to experience what the fast will be like. Most people will feel a little hungry at times and may experience a few mild symptoms such as headache, stomach rumbling, or irritability. These symptoms, however, depend on your state of toxicity. Usually, the first two days of fasting are the hardest for most people. Feeling great usually begins around the third day, so you will have a more grand experience the longer you stay on the fast.

One of the problems with fasting is that it can be the most difficult for those who need it the most, i.e., the regular three square-meals-plus-snacks a day person who eats whenever and whatever he or she wants. People in this category should start with simple diet changes and prepare even more slowly for their fast.

A transition plan to beginning the fast is the one- meal-a-day plan. The one daily meal should be eaten during the mid-afternoon at about 2:00 p.m. Water, fresh fruit or vegetable juices, and teas can be taken at other times of the day. The one wholesome meal should not be rich or excessive. It can be a vegetable meal, such as a salad and steamed vegetables, or a starch-vegetable meal, such as brown rice with mixed steamed greens, celery, carrots, and zucchini. People on this plan start to detoxify slowly, lose a bit of weight, and after a few days you will feel pretty good. The chance of any strong detoxification symptoms developing, as might occur with fasting, is minimal with this type of transition. Once the actual fast is begun, that experience will seem less severe, too.

The goal of the above transitional program is to help you to move into a four-day fast of raw vegetables and fruits building up to a five and ten day fast.

~~***~~

Chapter Six:
Combine the Right Foods

If I were asked the major cause of most illnesses, I would have to say incomplete digestion. If your food does not break down through the enzymes provided by fresh and raw food in your body, then putrefaction (rotting and decay) will take place. What is the result? Your body absorbs its own toxic waste before it can be eliminated. Have you ever tried doing two things at once? If you are anything like me, these tasks are usually rushed and incomplete. The same applies to your digestive process. If you combine the wrong foods together in a single meal, your body is required to process incompatible food substances at the same time, resulting in "incomplete digestion", discomfort, and putrefaction. Eating your meals as if they were a smorgasbord can only lead to disaster.

Food breaks down in the body with the aid of enzymes or bacteria. Enzyme breakdown is the natural course, while bacterial breakdown is quite destructive. Bacterial breakdown creates toxic gases which manifest in the body as bloating, burping, flatulence, Candida, fatigue, headaches, constipation, diarrhea, low back pain, etc. Your digestive tract will either be your highway to health, or to pain and suffering. You choose the road you want to take. We have been educated via media advertising to compromise our health for the heavenly tastes in the mouth with no concern for the following thirty feet of discomfort and/or pain that follows in our intestinal tract. Let's take a look at the concept of logical eating known as Food Combining.

THE REASON FOR PROPER FOOD COMBINING is to make digestion easier and more efficient. If you are going to eat more than one food at a meal, you can greatly improve digestion (and avoid indigestion)

39

by eating foods that are compatible and that require the same gastric juices for digestion. Properly combining foods leads to good digestion and to better health. "The simpler the meal the better you'll feel."

PROTEINS

Protein foods, or foods containing a high percentage of protein in their makeup, require an Acidic (low in oxygen) Digestive Environment. Chief among these are the following:

Nuts, Seeds	All flesh foods* (except fat)
Dry Beans	Dry Peas (combined as starches)
Eggs*	Cheese* and other dairy products*
Soy Beans	Peanuts
Margarine*	Chicken/Fish/Red Meat - AVOID PORK
Olives	Avocados

* These substances are not recommended, but are included for clarity.

CARBOHYDRATES The carbohydrates are the starches and sugars. These we break up into three distinct classifications: Starches, Sugars, and Sweet Fruits. Foods in these categories all require an Alkaline Digestive Environment (bicarbonate, further explained in chapter seven.).

STARCHES:	**SWEET FRUITS:**	**SUGARS:**	**MILDLY STARCHY:**
All Cereals	Prunes	Pure Honey*	Carrots
Dry Beans (except soy beans)	Persimmons	Pure Maple Syrup*	Artichokes
Dry Peas	Dried Fruits		Rutabaga
Potatoes	Bananas		Parsnips
Pumpkin	Dates		Beets
Yams	Figs		
Chestnuts	Raisins		
Squash			
Corn			
Coconut**			

* These foods are not recommended. ** Coconuts are a starch/protein combination and also a saturated fat.

GENERAL FOOD COMBINING GUIDELINES

Avoid eating carbohydrates with acid fruits

This combination may neutralize your enzymes causing your food to putrefy.

Avoid eating concentrated proteins with concentrated carbohydrates

Remember the pizza? How it made you feel? Especially when you were tired?

Do not consume two concentrated proteins at the same meal

Two concentrated proteins of different character and composition (such as nuts and cheese) should not be combined. Gastric acidity, type, strength, and timing of secretions for various proteins are not uniform. Since concentrated protein is more difficult to digest than other food elements, incompatible combinations of two different concentrated proteins should be avoided.

Do not consume fats with proteins

Our need for concentrated fat is small and most protein foods already contain a good deal of fat. Fat has an inhibiting effect on digestive secretions and lessens the amount and activity of pepsin and hydrochloric acid necessary for the digestion of protein. Fat may lower the entire digestive tone more than fifty percent.

Use fats sparingly

Fats inhibit the secretion of gastric juice. Except with avocado, fats used with starch delay the passage of the starch from the stomach into the intestine. When fats such as avocados or nuts are eaten with raw green vegetables, their inhibiting effect on gastric secretion is counteracted and digestion proceeds normally. **AVOCADOS:** Though not a high protein food, avocados contain more protein than milk. They are high in fat and the small percentage of protein they contain is of high biological value. They are best used with a salad meal. Eating avocados with salad enhances their digestibility. The next best combination for avocado is to take it with sub acid or acid fruit. It is even better when lettuce leaves and celery are eaten with the fruit and the avocado. Since the avocado is low in protein, it may also be used with potatoes or other starch foods, provided a green salad is included in the meal. Avocados should never be used with nuts, which are also high in fat. Fats other than nuts and avocados are not recommended for regular use.

Do not eat acid fruits with proteins

Citrus, tomatoes, pineapple, strawberries, and other acid fruits should not be eaten with nuts, cheese, eggs or meat. If you are ill, avoid acid fruits especially in juice form - but lemons and limes are always a great addition due to their enzyme content.

Do not combine sweet fruits with proteins, starches, or acid fruits

The sugars in sweet fruit should be free to leave the stomach within twenty minutes, and are apt to ferment if digestion is delayed by mixing with other foods. Sugar-starch combinations cause additional problems. When sugar is taken the mouth quickly fills with saliva, but no ptyalin is present. Ptyalin is essential for starch digestion. If starch is disguised by sugar, honey, molasses, or sweet fruit, digestion is impaired. Fermentation is inevitable if sugars of any kind are delayed in the stomach by the digestion of starch, protein, or acid fruit. Sugar also has a marked inhibiting effect on the flow of gastric juices.

Eat only one concentrated starch at a meal

This rule is more important as a means of avoiding overeating starches than avoiding a bad combination. Slightly starchy vegetables may be combined with more starchy vegetables such as carrots and potatoes, but not with combination foods such as grains and legumes.

Acid fruits may be used with sub acid fruits

This combination is best made with less sweet sub acid fruits. Never use acid fruits with sweet fruits. Tomatoes should neither be combined with sub acid fruit nor with any other kind of fruit. They are best combined with a salad or meal at which no starches are served. Sub acid fruits are fruits such as lemons.

Sub acid fruits may be used with sweet fruits

It is best to use the sweeter varieties of sub acid fruits when making this combination. For people with poor digestion, bananas are best eaten alone. For others, bananas combine fairly well with dates, raisins, grapes, and other sweet fruit, and with green leafy vegetables such as lettuce and celery. Dried sweet fruits should be used sparingly, because the sugar concentration is naturally greater. It is best to have these fruits at a fruit meal combined with a salad of lettuce and celery.

Combine fruit only with lettuce and celery

These uncooked vegetables with a fruit meal may even enhance digestion of the fruit.

Salads combine very well with proteins or starches

Non-starchy vegetables may be combined with proteins or starch. The green leafy vegetables combine very well with most other foods, and should form the major part of one's daily diet. Through the week, use as wide a variety of vegetables as possible. Lettuce and other green and non-starchy vegetables leave the stomach with little change. They pass through the stomach rapidly unless delayed by oily dressing or foods that require a more thorough gastric digestion.

Do not consume melons with any other foods

Many people who have complained that melons did not agree with them have no trouble when eating only melons at a meal. Melons are more than 90% liquid and leave the stomach quickly if not delayed and fermented by combining with other foods. Avoid over ripe fruit, this may cause digestive disturbances.

Sprouts

The best way to eat grains is as sprouts. When grains are sprouted, they come alive with enzymes and oxygen. They become a pre-digested food. Other seeds and legumes may be sprouted as well.

Water

You should drink alkaline water throughout the day. Do not allow your thirst to build up. Do not allow dehydration to occur. Do not drink a large amount at one time. It is better to have a smaller but continual flow of water for proper assimilation and detoxification. Don't dilute the natural enzymes in your body by drinking with meals. Water is a food; make it the best quality you can. Avoid chlorinated water for your health's sake, as it is known to be toxic.

References: For more information I recommend the following books: *Food Combining Made Easy* and *Superior Nutrition* by Herbert Shelton D.P., N.D., D.N.T, D.N.Sc. Excerpts from the above have been taken from a document published by The Canadian Natural Health Association Founded on Natural Hygiene, Toronto Chapter

From: Dr. Darrell L. Wolfe, The Wolfe Clinic

~~***~~

Chapter Seven:
Alkaline Your Body

Almost all foods that we eat, after being digested, absorbed, and metabolized, release either an acid or an alkaline base (bicarbonate) into the bloodstream. Grains, fish, meat, poultry, shellfish, cheese, milk, and salt all produce acid, so the introduction and dramatic rise in our consumption of these foods meant that the typical Western diet became more acid producing. The lack of fresh fruit and vegetables in our diet decreased the alkalinity, which further made the western diet acid producing.

Our blood is slightly alkaline, with a normal pH level of between 7.35 and 7.45. The theory behind the alkaline diet is that our diet should reflect this pH level (as it did in the past) and be slightly alkaline. Proponents of alkaline diets believe that a diet high in acid-producing foods disrupts this balance and promotes the loss of essential minerals such as potassium, magnesium, calcium, and sodium, as the body tries to restore equilibrium. This imbalance is thought to make people prone to illness.

Why Do People Try Alkaline Diets?

According to some alternative practitioners, the shift to an acid-producing diet is the cause of a number of chronic diseases. Most practitioners recommend the alkaline diet if a person has the following symptoms and other illnesses have been ruled out:

- Lack of energy

- Excessive mucous production

- Nasal congestion

Ray Morgan, OM.D. Ph.D.

- Frequent colds and flu
- Anxiety, nervousness, irritability
- Ovarian cysts, polycystic ovaries, benign breast cysts
- Headache

Although conventional doctors do believe that increasing consumption of fruit and vegetables and reducing one's intake of meat, salt, and refined grains is beneficial to health, most conventional doctors do not believe that an acid-producing diet is the foundation of chronic illness. In conventional medicine, there is evidence, however, that alkaline diets may help prevent the formation of calcium kidney stones, osteoporosis, and age-related muscle wasting.

What are the Safety Concerns?

It's a good idea to consult a competent medical professional (your doctor) before trying a new diet. The alkaline diet should not be used by people with acute or chronic kidney failure unless under a doctor's supervision. People with pre-existing heart disease and those on medications that affect potassium levels in the body should check with their doctor first.

How to Perform a Saliva pH Test

You can test your own pH level without the aid of a physician through a simple saliva test. The Saliva pH test measures your susceptibility to cancer, heart disease, osteoporosis, arthritis, and many other degenerative diseases. First, you must wait at least two hours after eating. Fill your mouth with saliva and then swallow it. Repeat this step to help ensure that your saliva is clean. Then the third time, put the pH saliva strip or paper on your tongue. The pH paper should turn blue. This indicates that your saliva is slightly alkaline at a healthy pH of 7.4. If it is not blue, compare the color with the chart that comes with the pH paper. If your saliva is acid (below pH of 7.0) wait two hours and repeat the test.

Where Can I Get pH Paper?

My favorite source for pH paper is my local Herb Shop. You should look for a narrow range pH paper measuring pH 4.5 to 7.5 or pH 4.5 to 8.5. Use these pH strips to measure acid/alkaline balance.

The Effect of Food on Urine pH

The list below categorizes a food as either acidic or alkaline based on the effect consumption of the food has on urine pH. For example, if a food tends to increase the acidity of urine after it is ingested, it is classified as an acid forming food. Conversely, if a food increases the alkalinity of urine after it has been ingested, it was classified it as an alkaline forming food. The effect foods have on urine pH may be quite different than the pH of the foods themselves. For example, orange juice is a highly acidic food due to its high citrus acid content, but after being metabolized it will cause urine to become alkaline. A urine test strip, similar to the saliva test strip, is available at your local drug store.

Most of the information below is based on information from my collection of nutrition books, including a chart I have from a Mayo Clinic diet manual, and also some from personal observations. The books I have all vary significantly in how they categorize the pH of different foods, so it is hard to tell which ones are correct. With this in mind, take the list below as a *general guide that most likely will contain some errors.*

It is interesting to note that the acid-base balance in the body can impact nutrient status. Researchers in Germany found that "acid-base status affects renal magnesium losses, irrespective of magnesium intake." This means that besides not eating enough foods high in magnesium, an acid load in the body could be another factor that contributes to magnesium deficiency.

Magnesium is a must. The diets of all Americans are likely to be deficient. Even a mild deficiency causes sensitivity to noise, nervousness, irritability, mental depression, confusion, twitching, trembling, apprehension, insomnia, muscle weakness and cramps in the toes, feet, legs, or fingers according to Adelle Davis, writing in *Let's Have Healthy Children.*

Shifting your pH toward Alkaline

This chart is for those trying to "adjust" their body pH. The pH scale is from 0 to 14, with numbers below 7 acidic (low on oxygen) and numbers above 7 alkaline. An acidic body is a sickness magnet. What you eat and drink will impact where your body's pH level falls. Balance is Key.

This chart is intended only as a general guide to alkalizing and acidifying foods.

...ALKALINE FOODS...	...ACIDIC FOODS...
ALKALIZING VEGETABLES	**ACIDIFYING VEGETABLES**
Alfalfa	Corn
Barley Grass	Lentils
Beet Greens	Olives
Beets	Winter Squash
Broccoli	
Cabbage	**ACIDIFYING FRUITS**
Carrot	Blueberries
Cauliflower	Canned or Glazed Fruits
Celery	Cranberries
Chard Greens	Currants
Chlorella	Plums**
Collard Greens	Prunes**
Cucumber	
Dandelions	**ACIDIFYING GRAINS, GRAIN**
Dulce	**PRODUCTS**
Edible Flowers	Amaranth
Eggplant	Barley
Fermented Veggies	Bran, oat
Garlic	Bran, wheat
Green Beans	Bread
Green Peas	Corn
Kale	Cornstarch
Kohlrabi	Crackers, soda
Lettuce	Flour, wheat
Mushrooms	Flour, white
Mustard Greens	Hemp Seed Flour
Nightshade Veggies	Kamut
Onions	Macaroni
Parsnips (high glycemic)	Noodles
Peas	Oatmeal
Peppers	Oats (rolled)
Pumpkin	Quinoa
Radishes	Rice (all)

Rutabaga
Sea Veggies
Spinach, green
Spirulina
Sprouts
Sweet Potatoes
Tomatoes
Watercress
Wheat Grass
Wild Greens

ALKALIZING ORIENTAL
VEGETABLES
Daikon
Dandelion Root
Kombu
Maitake
Nori
Reishi
Shitake
Umeboshi
Wakame

ALKALIZING FRUITS
Apple
Apricot
Avocado
Banana (high glycemic)
Berries
Blackberries
Cantaloupe
Cherries, sour
Coconut, fresh
Currants
Dates, dried
Figs, dried
Grapes
Grapefruit
Honeydew Melon
Lemon
Lime
Muskmelons

Rice Cakes
Rye
Spaghetti
Spelt
Wheat Germ
Wheat

ACIDIFYING BEANS & LEGUMES
Almond Milk
Black Beans
Chick Peas
Green Peas
Kidney Beans
Lentils
Pinto Beans
Red Beans
Rice Milk
Soy Beans
Soy Milk
White Beans

ACIDIFYING DAIRY
Butter
Cheese
Cheese, Processed
Ice Cream
Ice Milk

ACIDIFYING NUTS & BUTTERS
Cashews
Legumes
Peanut Butter
Peanuts
Pecans
Tahini
Walnuts

Nectarine
Orange
Peach
Pear
Pineapple
Raisins
Raspberries
Rhubarb
Strawberries
Tangerine
Tomato
Tropical Fruits
Umeboshi Plums
Watermelon

ALKALIZING PROTEIN
Almonds
Chestnuts
Millet
Tempeh (fermented)
Tofu (fermented)
Whey Protein Powder

ALKALIZING SWEETENERS
Stevia

ALKALIZING SPICES & SEASONINGS
Chili Pepper
Cinnamon
Curry
Ginger
Herbs (all)
Miso
Mustard
Sea Salt
Tamari

ACIDIFYING ANIMAL PROTEIN
Bacon
Beef
Carp
Clams
Cod
Corned Beef
Fish
Haddock
Lamb
Lobster
Mussels
Organ Meats
Oyster
Pike
Pork
Rabbit
Salmon
Sardines
Sausage
Scallops
Shellfish
Shrimp
Tuna
Turkey
Veal
Venison

ACIDIFYING FATS & OILS
Avocado Oil
Butter
Canola Oil
Corn Oil
Flax Oil
Hemp Seed Oil
Lard
Olive Oil
Safflower Oil
Sesame Oil
Sunflower Oil

ALKALIZING OTHER
Alkaline Antioxidant Water
Apple Cider Vinegar
Bee Pollen
Fresh Fruit Juice
Green Juices
Lecithin Granules
Mineral Water
Molasses, blackstrap
Probiotic Cultures
Soured Dairy Products
Veggie Juices

ALKALIZING MINERALS
Calcium: pH 12
Cesium: pH 14
Magnesium: pH 9
Potassium: pH 14
Sodium: pH 14

Although it might seem that citrus fruits would have an acidifying effect on the body, the citric acid they contain actually has an alkalinizing effect in the system.

Note that a food's acid or alkaline forming tendency in the body has nothing to do with the actual pH of the food itself. For example, lemons are very acidic, however the end products after digestion and assimilation are very alkaline so, lemons are alkaline forming in the body. Likewise, meat will test alkaline before digestion, but it leaves very acidic residue in the body so, as with nearly all animal products, meat is very acid forming.

ACIDIFYING SWEETENERS
Carob
Corn Syrup
Sugar

ACIDIFYING ALCOHOL
Beer
Hard Liquor
Spirits
Wine

ACIDIFYING OTHER FOODS
Catsup
Cocoa
Coffee
Mustard
Pepper
Soft Drinks
Vinegar

ACIDIFYING DRUGS & CHEMICALS
Aspirin
Chemicals
Drugs, Medicinal
Drugs, Psychedelic
Herbicides
Pesticides
Tobacco

ACIDIFYING JUNK FOOD
Beer: pH 2.5
Coca-Cola: pH 2
Coffee: pH 4

** These foods leave an alkaline ash but have an acidifying effect on the body.

Ray Morgan, OM.D. Ph.D.

UNKNOWN:
There are several versions of the Acidic and Alkaline Food chart to be found in different books and on the Internet. The following foods are sometimes attributed to the Acidic side of the chart and sometimes to the Alkaline side. Remember, you don't need to adhere strictly to the Alkaline side of the chart, just make sure a good percentage of the foods you eat come from that side.

Brazil Nuts	Maple Syrup
Brussels Sprouts	Milk
Buckwheat	Nuts
Cashews	Organic Milk (unpasteurized)
Chicken	Potatoes, white
Corn	Pumpkin Seeds
Cottage Cheese	Quinoa
Eggs	Sauerkraut
Flax Seeds	Soy Products
Green Tea	Sprouted Seeds
Herbal Tea	Squashes
Honey	Sunflower Seeds
Kombucha	Tomatoes
Lima Beans	Yogurt

* These statements have not been evaluated by the Food and Drug Administration and are not intended to diagnose, treat, cure, or prevent any disease; research is ongoing.

Here's a chart that ranks foods from most alkaline to most acidic.

Ranked Foods: Alkaline to Acidic

Extremely Alkaline
Lemons, watermelon.

Alkaline Forming
Cantaloupe, cayenne celery, dates, figs, kelp, limes, mango, melons, papaya, parsley, seaweeds, seedless grapes (sweet), watercress.
Asparagus, fruit juices, grapes (sweet), kiwifruit, passion fruit, pears (sweet), pineapple, raisins, umeboshi plums, and vegetable juices.

Moderately Alkaline
Apples (sweet), alfalfa sprouts, apricots, avocados, bananas (ripe), currants, dates, figs (fresh), garlic, grapefruit, grapes (less sweet), guavas, herbs (leafy green), lettuce (leafy green), nectarine, peaches (sweet), pears (less sweet), peas (fresh, sweet), pumpkin (sweet), sea salt (vegetable).

Apples (sour), beans (fresh, green), beets, bell peppers, broccoli, cabbage, carob, cauliflower, ginger (fresh), grapes (sour), lettuce (pale green), oranges, peaches (less sweet), peas (less sweet), potatoes (with skin), pumpkin (less sweet), raspberries, strawberries, squash, sweet Corn (fresh), turnip, vinegar (apple cider).

Slightly Alkaline
Almonds, Jerusalem artichokes, brussels sprouts, cherries, coconut (fresh), cucumbers, eggplant, honey (raw), leeks, mushrooms, okra, olives (ripe), onions, pickles (homemade), radishes, sea salt, spices, tomatoes (sweet), vinegar (sweet brown rice).

Chestnuts (dry, roasted), egg yolks (soft cooked), essene bread, goat's milk and whey (raw), mayonnaise (homemade), olive oil, sesame seeds (whole), soy beans (dry), soy cheese, soymilk, sprouted grains, tofu, tomatoes (less sweet), and yeast (nutritional flakes).

Neutral
Butter (fresh, unsalted), cream (fresh, raw), cow's milk and whey (raw), margarine, oils (except olive), and yogurt (plain).

Moderately Acidic
Bananas (green), barley (rye), blueberries, bran, butter, cereals (unrefined), cheeses, crackers (unrefined rye, rice and wheat), cranberries, dried beans (mung, adzuki, pinto, kidney, garbanzo), dry coconut, egg whites, eggs whole (cooked hard), fructose, goat's milk (homogenized), honey (pasteurized), ketchup, maple syrup (unprocessed), milk (homogenized).

Molasses (unsulfered and organic), most nuts, mustard, oats (rye, organic), olives (pickled), pasta (whole grain), pastry (whole grain and honey), plums, popcorn (with salt and/or butter), potatoes, prunes, rice (basmati and brown), seeds (pumpkin, sunflower), soy sauce, and wheat bread (sprouted organic).

Extremely Acidic
Artificial sweeteners, beef, beer, breads, brown sugar, carbonated soft drinks, cereals (refined), chocolate, cigarettes and tobacco, coffee, cream of wheat (unrefined), custard (with white sugar), deer, drugs, fish, flour (white, wheat), fruit juices with sugar, jams, jellies, lamb.

Liquor, maple syrup (processed), molasses (unsulphured), pasta (white), pastries and cakes from white flour, pickles (commercial), pork, poultry, seafood, sugar (white), table salt (refined and iodized), tea (black), white bread, white vinegar (processed), whole wheat foods, wine, and yogurt (sweetened).

More Ranked Foods: Alkaline to Acidic

Highly Alkaline Forming Foods
Baking soda, sea salt, mineral water, pumpkin seed, lentils, seaweed, onion, taro root, sea vegetables, lotus root, sweet potato, lime, lemons, nectarine, persimmon, raspberry, watermelon, tangerine, and pineapple.

Moderately Alkaline Forming Foods
Apricots, spices, kombucha, unsulfured molasses, soy sauce, cashews, chestnuts, pepper, kohlrabi, parsnip, garlic, asparagus, kale, parsley, endive, arugula, mustard green, ginger root, broccoli, grapefruit, cantaloupe, honeydew, citrus, olive, dewberry, carrots, loganberry, and mango.

Low Alkaline Forming Foods
Most herbs, green tea, mu tea, rice syrup, apple cider vinegar, sake, quail eggs, primrose oil, sesame seed, cod liver oil, almonds, sprouts, potato, bell pepper, mushrooms, cauliflower, cabbage, rutabaga, ginseng, eggplant, pumpkin, collard green, pear, avocado, apples (sour), blackberry, cherry, peach, and papaya.

Very Low Alkaline Forming Foods
Ginger tea, umeboshi vinegar, ghee, duck eggs, oats, grain coffee, quinoa, japonica rice, wild rice, avocado oil, most seeds, coconut oil, olive oil, flax oil, brussels sprout, beet, chive, cilantro, celery, okra, cucumber, turnip greens, squashes, lettuces, orange, banana, blueberry, raisin, currant, grape, and strawberry.

Very Low Acid Forming Foods
Curry, koma coffee, honey, maple syrup, vinegar, cream, butter, goat/sheep cheese, chicken, gelatin, organs, venison, fish, wild duck, triticale, millet, kasha, amaranth, brown rice, pumpkin seed oil, grape seed oil, sunflower oil, pine nuts, canola oil, spinach, fava beans, black-eyed peas, string beans, wax beans, zucchini, chutney, rhubarb, coconut, guava, dry fruit, figs, and dates.

Low Acid Forming Foods
Vanilla, alcohol, black tea, balsamic vinegar, cow milk, aged cheese, soy cheese, goat milk, game meat, lamb, mutton, boar, elk, shell fish, mollusks, goose, turkey, buckwheat, wheat, spelt, teff, kamut, farina, semolina, white rice, almond oil, sesame oil, safflower oil, tapioca, seitan, tofu, pinto beans, white beans, navy beans, red beans, aduki beans, lima beans, chard, plum, prune and tomatoes.

Moderately Acid Forming Foods
Nutmeg, coffee, casein, milk protein, cottage cheese, soy milk, pork, veal, bear, mussels, squid, chicken, maize, barley groats, corn, rye, oat bran, pistachio seeds, chestnut oil, lard, pecans, palm kernel oil, green peas, peanuts, snow peas, other legumes, garbanzo beans, cranberry, and pomegranate.

Highly Acid Forming Foods
Tabletop sweeteners like (NutraSweet, Spoonful, Sweet 'N Low, Equal or
Aspartame), pudding, jam, jelly, table salt (NaCl), beer, yeast, hops, malt, sugar,
cocoa, white (acetic acid) vinegar, processed cheese, ice cream, beef, lobster,
pheasant, barley, cottonseed oil, hazelnuts, walnuts, brazil nuts, fried foods,
soybean, and soft drinks, especially the cola type. To neutralize a glass of cola
with a pH of 2.5, it would take 32 glasses of alkaline water with a pH of 10.

Ray Morgan, OM.D. Ph.D.

A list of Acid / Alkaline Forming Foods

Alkaline Forming Foods
VEGETABLES
Garlic
Asparagus
Fermented Veggies
Watercress
Beets
Broccoli
Brussels sprouts
Cabbage
Carrot
Cauliflower
Celery
Chard
Chlorella
Collard Greens
Cucumber
Eggplant
Kale
Kohlrabi
Lettuce
Mushrooms
Mustard Greens
Dulce
Dandelions
Edible Flowers
Onions
Parsnips (high glycemic)
Peas
Peppers
Pumpkin
Rutabaga
Miso
Tamari
All Herbs
Sea Veggies
Spirulina
Sprouts
Squashes
Alfalfa
Barley Grass

Acid Forming Foods
FATS & OILS
Avocado Oil
Canola Oil
Corn Oil
Hemp Seed Oil
Flax Oil
Lard
Olive Oil
Safflower Oil
Sesame Oil
Sunflower Oil
FRUITS
Cranberries
GRAINS
Rice Cakes
Wheat Cakes
Amaranth
Barley
Buck-wheat
Corn
Oats (rolled)
Quinoa
Rice (all)
Rye
Spelt
Kamut
Wheat
Hemp Seed Flour

DAIRY
Cheese, Cow
Cheese, Goat
Cheese, Processed
Cheese, Sheep
Milk
Butter

Wheat Grass
Wild Greens
Nightshade Veggies
FRUITS
Apple
Apricot
Avocado
Banana (high glycemic)
Cantaloupe
Cherries
Currants
Dates/Figs
Grapes
Grapefruit
Lime
Honeydew Melon
Nectarine
Orange
Lemon
Peach
Pear
Pineapple
All Berries
Tangerine
Tomato
Tropical Fruits
Watermelon

PROTEIN
Eggs (poached)
Whey Protein Powder
Cottage Cheese
Chicken Breast
Yogurt
Almonds
Chestnuts
Tofu (fermented)
Flax Seeds
Pumpkin Seeds
Tempeh (fermented)
Squash Seeds
Sunflower Seeds
Millet
Sprouted Seeds
Nuts

NUTS & BUTTERS
Cashews
Brazil Nuts
Peanuts
Peanut Butter
Pecans
Tahini
Walnuts

ANIMAL PROTEIN
Beef
Carp
Clams
Fish
Lamb
Lobster
Mussels
Oyster
Pork
Rabbit
Salmon
Shrimp
Scallops
Tuna
Turkey
Venison

PASTA (WHITE)
Noodles
Macaroni
Spaghetti

OTHER
Distilled Vinegar
Wheat Germ
Potatoes

DRUGS & CHEMICALS
Aspartame
Chemicals
Drugs, Medicinal
Drugs, Psychedelic
Pesticides
Herbicides

Ray Morgan, OM.D. Ph.D.

OTHER
Apple Cider Vinegar
Bee Pollen
Lecithin Granules
Probiotic Cultures
Green Juices
Veggies Juices
Fresh Fruit Juice
Organic Milk
(unpasteurized)
Mineral Water
Alkaline Antioxidant Water
Green Tea
Herbal Tea
Dandelion Tea
Ginseng Tea
Banchi Tea
Kombucha

SWEETENERS
Stevia
Ki Sweet

SPICES/SEASONINGS
Cinnamon
Curry
Ginger
Mustard
Chili Pepper
Sea Salt

ORIENTAL VEGETABLES
Maitake
Daikon
Dandelion Root
Shitake
Kombu
Reishi
Nori
Umeboshi
Wakame
Sea Veggies

ALCOHOL
Beer
Spirits
Hard Liquor
Wine

BEANS & LEGUMES
Black Beans
Chick Peas
Green Peas
Kidney Beans
Lentils
Lima Beans
Pinto Beans
Red Beans
Soy Beans
Soy Milk
White Beans
Rice Milk
Almond Milk

More Ranked Foods: Alkaline (pH) to Acidic (pH)

Alkaline: Meditation, Prayer, Peace, Kindness & Love

Extremely Alkaline Forming Foods - pH 8.5 to 9.0

9.0 Lemons **1,** Watermelon **2**

8.5 Agar **3,** Cantaloupe, Cayenne (Capsicum) **4,**

Dried dates & figs, Kelp, Karengo, Kudzu root, Limes,

Mango, Melons, Papaya, Parsley **5,** Seedless grapes

(sweet), Watercress, Seaweeds

Asparagus **6,** Endive, Kiwifruit, Fruit juices **7,** Grapes

(sweet), Passion fruit, Pears (sweet), Pineapple,

Raisins, Umeboshi plum, Vegetable juices **8**

Moderate Alkaline - pH 7.5 to 8.0

Acid: Overwork, Anger, Fear, Jealousy & Stress

Extremely Acid Forming Foods - pH 5.0 to 5.5

5.0 Artificial sweeteners

5.5 Beef, Carbonated soft drinks & fizzy drinks **38,**
Cigarettes (tailor made), Drugs, Flour (white, wheat)
39, Goat, Lamb, Pastries & cakes from white flour,
Pork, Sugar (white) **40**
Beer **34,** Brown sugar **35,** Chicken, Deer, Chocolate,
Coffee **36,** Custard with white sugar, Jams, Jellies,
Liquor **37,** Pasta (white), Rabbit, Semolina, Table
salt refined and iodized, Tea black, Turkey, Wheat
bread, White rice, White vinegar (processed).

Moderate Acid - pH 6.0 to 6.5

8.0 Apples (sweet), Apricots, Alfalfa sprouts **9,**
Arrowroot, Flour **10,** Avocados, Bananas (ripe),
Berries, Carrots, Celery, Currants, Dates & figs
(fresh), Garlic **11,** Gooseberry, Grapes (less sweet),
Grapefruit, Guavas, Herbs (leafy green), Lettuce
(leafy green), Nectarine, Peaches (sweet), Pears
(less sweet), Peas (fresh sweet), Persimmon,
Pumpkin (sweet), Sea salt (vegetable) **12,** Spinach

7.5 Apples (sour), Bamboo shoots, Beans (fresh green),
Beets, Bell Pepper, Broccoli, Cabbage; Cauliflower, Carob
13, Daikon, Ginger (fresh), Grapes (sour), Kale,
Kohlrabi, Lettuce (pale green), Oranges, Parsnip,
Peaches (less sweet), Peas (less sweet), Potatoes
& skin, Pumpkin (less sweet), Raspberry, Sapote,
Strawberry, Squash **14,** Sweet corn (fresh), Tamari
15, Turnip, Vinegar (apple cider) **16**

Slightly Alkaline to Neutral pH 7.0

6.0 Cigarette tobacco (roll your own), Cream of Wheat
(unrefined), Fish, Fruit juices with sugar, Maple
syrup (processed), Molasses (sculptured), Pickles
(commercial), Breads (refined) of corn, oats, rice &
rye, Cereals (refined) e.g. sweatbox, corn flakes,
Shellfish, Wheat germ, Whole Wheat foods **32,**
Wine **33,** Yogurt (sweetened)

6.5 Bananas (green), Buckwheat, Cheeses (sharp),
Corn & rice breads, Egg whole (cooked hard),
Ketchup, Mayonnaise, Oats, Pasta (whole grain),
Pastry (wholegrain & honey), Peanuts, Potatoes
 (with no skins), Popcorn (with salt & butter), Rice
 (basmati), Rice (brown), Soy sauce (commercial),
Tapioca, Wheat bread (sprouted organic)

Slightly Acid to Neutral pH 7.0

7.0 Almonds **17,** Artichokes (Jerusalem), Barley-Malt (sweetener-Brunner), Brown Rice Syrup, Brussels Sprouts, Cherries, Coconut (fresh), Cucumbers, Egg plant, Honey (raw), Leeks, Milo, Mushrooms, Okra, Olives ripe **18,** Onions, Pickles **19,** (home made), Radish, Sea salt **20,** Spices **21,** Taro, Tomatoes (sweet), Vinegar (sweet brown rice), Water Chestnut Amaranth, Artichoke (globe), Chestnuts (dry roasted), Egg yolks (soft cooked), Essene bread **22,** Goat's milk and whey (raw) **23,** Horseradish, Mayonnaise (home made), Millet, Olive oil, Quinoa, Rhubarb, Sesame seeds (whole) **24,** Soy beans (dry), Soy cheese, Soy milk, Sprouted grains **25,** empeh, Tofu, Tomatoes (less sweet), Yeast (nutritional flakes)

7.0 Barley malt syrup, Barley, Bran, Cashews, Cereals (unrefined with honey-fruit-maple syrup), Cornmeal, Cranberries **30,** Fructose, Honey (pasteurized), Lentils, Macadamias, Maple syrup (unprocessed), Milk (homogenized) and most processed dairy products, Molasses (unsulphered organic) **31,** Nutmeg, Mustard, Pistachios, Popcorn & butter (plain), Rice or wheat crackers (unrefined), Rye (grain), Rye bread (organic sprouted), Seeds (pumpkin & sunflower), Walnuts Blueberries, Brazil nuts, Butter (salted), Cheeses (mild & crumbly) **28,** Crackers (unrefined rye), Dried beans (mung, adzuki, pinto, kidney, garbanzo) **29,** Dry coconut, Egg whites, Goats milk (homogenized), Olives (pickled), Pecans, Plums **30,** Prunes **30,** Spelt

Neutral pH 7.0 ‹ Healthy Body Saliva pH Range is between 6.4 to 6.8 (on your pH test strips)

Butter (fresh unsalted), Cream (fresh and raw), Margarine **26,** Milk (raw cow's) **27,** Oils (except olive), Whey (cow's), Yogurt (plain)

Ray Morgan, OM.D. Ph.D.

NOTE: Match with the numbers above.
1. Excellent for *EMERGENCY SUPPORT* for colds, coughs, sore throats, heartburn, and gastro upsets.
2. Good for a yearly fast. For several days eat whole melon, chew pips well and eat also. Super alkalizing food.
3. Substitute for gelatin, more nourishing.
4. Stimulating, non-irritating body healer. Good for endocrine system.
5. Purifies kidneys.
6. Powerful acid reducer detoxing to produce acid urine temporarily, causing alkalinity for the long term.
7. Natural sugars give alkalinity. Added sugar causes juice to become acid forming.
8. Depends on vegetable's content and sweetness.
9. Enzyme rich, superior digestibility.
10. High calcium content. Cornflour substitute.
11. Elevates acid food 5.0 in alkaline direction.
12. Vegetable content raises alkalinity.
13. Substitute for coca; mineral rich.
14. Winter squash rates 7.5. Butternut and sweeter squash rates 8.0.
15. Genuine fermented for 1 1/2 years otherwise 6.0.
16. Raw unpasteurized is a digestive aid to increase HCL in the stomach. 1 tablespoon, + honey & water before meals.
17. Soak 12 hours, peel skin to eat.
18. Sundried, tree ripened, otherwise 6.0.
19. Using sea salt and apple cider vinegar.
20. Contains sea minerals. Dried at low temperatures.
21. Range from 7.0 to 8.0.
22. Sprouted grains are more alkaline. Grains chewed well become more alkaline.
23. High sodium to aid digestion.
24. High levels of utilizable calcium. Grind before eating.
25. Alkalinity and digestibility higher.
26. Heating causes fats to harden and become indigestible.
27. High mucus production.**28**. Mucus forming and hard to digest.
29. When sprouted dry beans rate 7.0.
30. Contain acid-forming benzoic and quinic acids.
31. Full of iron.
32. Unrefined wheat is more alkaline.
33. High quality red wine, no more than 4 oz. daily to build blood.
34. Good quality, well brewed - up to 5.5. Fast brewed beers drop to 5.0.
35. Most are white sugars with golden syrup added.
36. Organic, fresh ground-up to 5.5.
37. Cheaper brands drop to 5.0, as does over-indulgence.
38. Leaches minerals.
39. Bleached - has no health benefits.
40. Poison! Avoid it.
41. Potential cancer agent. Over-indulgence may cause partial blindness.

I get a lot of emails from people saying distilled water is not acidic or that it is very healthy for you to drink. According to the Environmental Protection web site, "Pure distilled water would have tested neutral, but pure distilled water is not easily obtained because carbon dioxide in the air around us mixes, or dissolves, in the water, making it somewhat acidic. The pH of distilled water is between 5.6 and 7. The pH of distilled water I have bought from stores and tested myself at home has always tested out to be acidic.

Alkaline Foods - Acidic Foods

Overview

Very Acidic Foods and Supplements Include:

- Eggs

- Liver and other organ meats

- Gravy

- Broth made from bones or other animal parts

- Wine

- Yogurt with active cultures

- Buttermilk, including buttermilk pancakes and biscuits

- Sour cream

- Most fermented foods and aged cheeses

- Some B vitamin supplements (or foods supplemented with B vitamins) can make your stomach more acid

- Hydrochloric acid supplements

- Digestive enzymes

Please note that fermented foods like yogurt, buttermilk, and sour cream seem to become more acidic in the body if they contain some types of active cultures of helpful bacteria.

Ray Morgan, OM.D. Ph.D.

Non-Food Substances That Can Make Urine Acidic

- **Probiotics** - These are supplements that contain "helpful bacteria." At least some types of beneficial bacteria help to create an acidic environment in the digestive tract. Probiotics are often used after taking antibiotics and may help some cases of bladder infections, irritable bowel syndrome and diarrhea. My friends and family have noticed that if we take excess amounts of probiotics it may cause heartburn and/or high blood pressure.

- **Soft water** - Soft water is water that is low in minerals. This type of water tends to be more acidic.

Alkaline Foods

- Most fruits, except as noted above
- Most vegetables, except as noted above

Very Alkaline Foods Include

- Bananas
- Chocolate
- Figs
- Mineral water
- Orange juice
- Potatoes
- Spinach
- Watermelon
- Dandelion Greens

Please note that some foods, such as citrus fruits, have an acid pH before they are consumed and but they usually leave an alkaline residue in the body after they have been metabolized. Sorry to restate this twice, but I am frequently questioned on this particular topic.

Non-Food Substances That Can Make Urine Alkaline

- **Antibiotics** - antibiotics destroy both the bad and the helpful bacteria in the intestinal tract. Some of the helpful bacteria work to create an acidic environment in the human body. When these bacteria are eliminated by antibiotics, urine may become more alkaline. I think this is one reason why women frequently get bladder infections after taking antibiotics.

- I have some old nutrition textbooks, and in the era before widespread antibiotic use, health care professionals often advised people suffering from urinary tract infections to eat a lot of meat and other acid forming foods. Many allopathic doctors of today think acid-base balance is a lot of malarkey, but thirty years ago you could actually find this type of knowledge in some college nutrition text books.

- **Many mineral supplements** - especially calcium, potassium, iron and magnesium. Calcium and magnesium are common ingredients in antacids as they neutralize stomach acid. Some people get upset stomachs (gas, bloating, diarrhea, malabsorption) from these types of mineral supplements, especially if they suffer from hypochloridia (low stomach acid).

- **Antacids** - Antacids, which often contain magnesium or calcium supplements, may cause an increase in the alkalinity of the urine, which can lead to bladder infections as bacteria tend to thrive in alkaline environments.

- **Hard Water** - Hard water is just the opposite of soft water. It is water that has a high mineral content, and as a result tends to be more alkaline._Some studies have shown that people have fewer heart attacks where the water is hard, presumably because the dissolved minerals that make the water hard are important for nutrition.

Neutral Foods

The Mayo Clinic Diet Manual, Seventh Edition categorizes the following foods as neutral foods: My recommendation is to proceed with caution:

- Butter

- Margarine

- Cooking fats

- Oils

- Plain candies

- Sugar

- Syrup

- Honey

- Arrowroot

- Corn

- Tapioca

- Coffee

- Tea

Many other books on pH balance have conflicting information to the neutral foods listed above. Most alternative health books I own state that coffee; tea, sugar (and anything with sugar), and corn make the urine more acid.

"Let nothing which can be treated by diet be treated by other means." Maimonides

Healing with Probiotics

A *probiotic* is an organism which contributes to the health and balance of the intestinal tract. A probiotic is also referred to as the "friendly," "beneficial," or "good" bacteria which when ingested act to maintain a healthy intestinal tract and help fight illness and disease. Most of us are not aware there are twenty times more bacteria than cells in our body. In fact, at any one time, you have more bacteria in your body than the total number of people who have ever lived on the planet. So the next time you step on the bathroom scale, you need to remember that one pound of that weight is not you at all, but the billions of bugs that live in your gut. This may sound alarming, but many of these organisms are crucial to good health.

A healthy lower intestine should contain at least 85% friendly bacteria to prevent the over colonization of disease-causing micro-organisms like E. coli and salmonella. Our colon can maintain its health with 15% unfriendly bacteria if the body contains at least 85% probiotic friendly bacteria. Most people have this balance. The word probiotic simply means "for life," which explains why these nutrients are so important. Here is the scientific definition of a probiotic: "A live microbial feed supplement, which beneficially affects the host by improving its intestinal microbial balance."

New research is establishing how important the supplementation of probiotics can be for a variety of conditions. For instance, probiotics enhance the immune system by favorably altering the gut micro-ecology and preventing unfriendly organisms from gaining a foothold in the body. They prevent the overgrowth of yeast and fungus and produce substances that can lower cholesterol.

Probiotics are widely recommended for the treatment of Candida, a fungal infection, because they establish large, healthy populations of friendly bacteria that compete with the candida that is trying to take up residence in the intestine. Probiotics are also essential in the treatment and prevention of thrush, vaginal yeast infections, and athlete's foot. Good health depends fundamentally upon the more than 400 types of friendly, symbiotic bacteria that inhabit the digestive tract.

Why Do We Need Probiotics?

Two of the most damaging substances to the delicate intestinal flora balance are chlorine and sodium fluoride, present in most treated municipal water, and thus also present in most beverages that one gets at restaurants. The drinking of alcoholic beverages also contributes to the destruction of the intestinal flora. Medical antibiotics, birth control pills and many other allopathic drugs cause damage to the intestinal flora and to the tissue in the intestinal wall.

Poor eating habits, chlorinated drinking water, stress, disease, and the use of antibiotics in food production as well as in medical treatments, can wreak havoc in the gastrointestinal tract by destroying good bacteria and allowing undesirable bacteria to multiply. When the ratio of good bacteria to bad is lowered, problems begin to arise such as excessive gas, bloating, constipation, intestinal toxicity, and poor absorption of nutrients.

~~***~~

Chapter Eight:
Cleanse Your Kidneys

Did you know that your chances of developing a kidney stone in your lifetime are one in ten? More than 300,000 people in America suffer from renal failure each year and undergo dialysis or await a kidney transplant. As I write this, one of my very close friends called to inform me that he has stage four renal failure and is a candidate for dialysis. His doctor plans to add his name to the registry for kidney transplant candidates.

Your kidneys are two bean-shaped organs, each about the size of your fist. Although the kidneys are small organs by weight, they receive approximately 20% of the blood pumped by the heart. Every day, your kidneys process about 200 quarts of blood to sift out about two quarts of waste products and extra water.

The actual filtering occurs in tiny units inside your kidneys called *nephrons*. Every kidney has about a million nephrons. In the nephron, a *glomerulus* — which is a tiny blood vessel, or capillary — intertwines with a tiny urine-collecting tube called a tubule. A complicated chemical exchange takes place, as waste materials and water leave your blood and enter your urinary system. The large blood supply to your kidneys enables them to do the following tasks:

Your kidneys receive the blood, remove waste from the blood, and then return the processed blood to the body. The unwanted substances end up in the urine. Urine flows from the kidneys to the bladder through the urethra. The *urethra* is a tube that connects the urinary bladder to the genitals for removal out of the body. They also:

- Regulate the composition of your blood.

- Keep constant the concentrations of various ions and other important substances.

- Keep constant the volume of water in your body.

- Remove wastes from your body (urea, drugs, toxic substances).

- Keep the acid base concentration of your blood constant.

- Help regulate your blood pressure.

- Stimulate the production of red blood cells.

- Maintain your body's calcium levels.

You cannot live without adequately functioning kidneys and liver. Therefore, it may be necessary for your doctor to run some of the following tests periodically to determine whether these vital organs are functioning sufficiently.

The following series of tests may be necessary to determine the health of your kidneys.

Please refer to the references chart below for a more complete description of various tests.

BUN (Blood Urea Nitrogen or Urea Nitrogen). This is the concentration of nitrogen (within urea) in the serum (but not in red blood cells). It's a waste product, derived from protein breakdown, produced in the liver and excreted by way of the kidneys. High values may mean that the kidneys are not working as well as they should. BUN is also elevated by blood loss, dehydration, high protein diets and/or strenuous exercise which may temporarily and artificially raise levels. A low BUN level may be the result of liver disease, or a low protein diet.

Creatinine. Creatinine is waste product largely from muscle metabolism (breakdown). Concentration of creatinine in the blood depends upon the amount of muscle that you have and the ability of your kidneys to excrete creatinine. High values, especially with high BUN levels, may indicate problems with the kidneys. Low values are generally not considered significant.

Calcium. Calcium is one of the most important elements in the body. The parathyroid gland and the kidneys control the amount of calcium in the blood. The parathyroid gland is the main regulator of calcium in the body. Nearly all of the calcium in the body is found in bone (99%). The remaining 1% is very important for proper clotting, and nerve, cell and enzyme activity. An elevated calcium level can be due to medication (such as too much calcitriol-synthetic vitamin D), inherited disorders of calcium handling in the kidneys, bone disease, or excess parathyroid gland activity or vitamin D. Low calcium can be due to malnutrition, drugs and certain metabolic disorders.

Sodium. An electrolyte regulated by the kidneys and adrenal glands. This element plays an important role in the water/salt balance in your body.

Potassium. Potassium is an electrolyte found primarily inside cells and must be controlled very carefully by the kidneys. Its role is to maintain water balance inside the cells and to help in the transmission of nerve impulses. A low potassium level can cause muscle weakness and heart problems. A high potassium level can be found in kidney disease or in over ingestion of potassium supplements.

Chloride. Chloride is an electrolyte regulated by the kidneys and adrenal glands. Chloride is important to the function of nerves, muscles, and cells. It is usually associated with a high or low level of sodium or potassium.

CO2. Co2 levels reflect the acid status of your blood. See the references listed under (2) for details on the cause of high or low levels. Corticosteriods as well as kidney disease can be involved.

BUN/Creatinine Ratio - This ratio is sometimes used for diagnostic purposes.

Example Complete Metabolic Panel

Note: the yellow area highlights kidney function tests. Reference ranges may vary from laboratory to laboratory. HI and LO are relative to the Reference Range.

Typical Complete Metabolic Panel - Blood Tests

Ray Morgan, OM.D. Ph.D.

Test	Flag, LO=Low, HI= High	Result	Units	Reference Range[4]
Sodium	LO	136.	mmol/L	137 - 145
Potassium		4.0	mmol/L	3.6 - 5.0
Chloride		103.	mmol/L	98. - 107.
CO2		30.	mmol/L	22. - 31.
Alkaline Phosphate		39.	U/L	38. - 126.
Total Bilirubin		0.3	mg/dL	.2 - 1.3
AST	HI	67.	U/L	8. - 50.
ALT	HI	104.	U/L	9. - 72.
Albumin	LO	3.4	g/dL	3.9 - 5.0
Total Protein		6.8	g/dL	6.3 - 8.2
Creatinine (*)		1.0	mg/dL	0.7 - 1.5
Urea Nitrogen (BUN)		18.	mg/dL	7.0 - 20.
Calcium		9.1	mg/dL	8.4 - 10.2
Glucose		92.	mg/dL	65. - 110.
LDH		516	U/L	313 - 618

(*) Units of μmol/L result in a reference range, for example, of 70-120 μmol/L.

References

1. D. Nicoli et al, *Pocket Guide to* Diagnostic Tests, 3rd edition, McGraw-Hill 2001.

An easy way to help your kidney each day is to purchase a few huge watermelons and eat as much of them as you can throughout the day, while regularly emptying your bladder. When kidneys or bladder are ill, gradually increase the amount of watermelon you are consuming. Be sure to start as slowly as possible to avoid feeling pressure in the bladder. You can do yourself a lot of good by initiating the following kidney and bladder flush at the change of each season:

Kidney and Bladder Flush Ingredients:

Each Day for Five Days:

When you wake up, drink eight ounces of distilled water. It is actually recommended that you always drink water the first thing in the morning, as this will flush leftover food and unneeded digestive juices out of your digestive tract.

One hour after the water, prepare and drink the *flush* (also called the *Master Cleanse)* using this recipe:

- Squeeze the juices of one lemon and one lime

- Combine the lemon and lime juices with 20 oz. of distilled water utilizing a blender

- Add a pinch of cayenne pepper, please start very slowly with this

- Optional – Add some Agave nectar (just a little) to taste

One-half hour after the kidney and bladder flush, begin the kidney cleanse.

Kidney and Bladder Cleanse

- One-half cup dried Hydrangea Root (Hydrangea arborescens)

- One-half cup Gravel Root (Eupatorium purpureum)

- One-half cup Marshmallow Root (Althea officinallis)

- Black Cherry Concentrate, 8 oz. (twice)

- Pinch of vitamin B2 powder

- 4 bunches of fresh parsley (a bunch at stems is about 2 inches)

- Goldenrod tincture (leave out of the recipe if you are allergic to it)

- Ginger root, Uva Ursi (A small piece)

- Vitamin B6, 250 mg caps

- Magnesium oxide, 300 mg caps

- HCl drops (Hydrochloric Acid) Sweetening is optional; if you must sweeten the mixture - use Agave Nectar

Previous versions of this recipe included vegetable glycerin. Recently I have been unable to find a source free from asbestos and silicone. So please omit glycerin.

Measure 1/4 (one fourth) cup of each root [half of the roots] and set them to soak, together in 10 cups of room temperature distilled water, using a glass container with a glass lid. Add vitamin B2 powder. After four hours (or overnight), heat to boiling and simmer for 20 minutes. Remove from heat, add 8 oz. of black cherry concentrate and bring back to boiling. Pour through a bamboo or plastic strainer into glass jar, stir in two drops of HCI. Drink 3/4 (three fourths) of a cup by sipping slowly throughout the day. Refrigerate half to use this week, and freeze the other half for next week.

Other versions of this recipe allowed re-boiling of the roots when you have finished your first batch. Although this saves a few dollars, you should use a new batch of herbs each time. You need to do the kidney cleanse for six weeks to get the needed results, but do it longer for severe problems.

Find fresh parsley at a grocery store. Soak it in HCl-water (use one drop per cup) with a pinch of vitamin B2 in it for two minutes. Drain. Cover with two pints of distilled water and boil for one minute. Drain into a glass jar. When cool enough, pour for yourself 1/2 cup. Add two drops HCL. Sip slowly or add to your root potion. Refrigerate a pint and freeze one pint for next week. Throw away the parsley. Always add two drops of HCl before drinking even after pre-sterilizing.

Dose: Each morning, pour together 3/4 (three fourths) of a cup of the root mixture and 1/2 cup parsley water, filling a large mug. Add 20 drops of goldenrod tincture and any spice, such as nutmeg, cinnamon, etc. Then add a pinch of Vitamin B2 and B4 drops. Use the HCl to sterilize. Drink this mixture in divided doses throughout the day. Keep it cold. Do not drink it all at once or you will get a stomach ache and feel pressure in your bladder. If your stomach is very sensitive, start with half the dose.

Breakfast:

Fresh fruit or fresh vegetable juice should complement your recommended dosages of vitamins, minerals and other essential nutrients, for they also deliver important detoxification and cleansing benefits. Should you find yourself hungry before lunch, you may opt to have a piece of fruit, a glass of diluted fruit juice, or a fruit smoothie. You will, however, need to stop drinking fruit juice a minimum of one hour before lunch. Remember that while following this program, it is best not to combine fruit and vegetables within a single meal. Fruits and fruit juice should always be eaten alone.

Lunch and Dinner: should consist of vegetables or vegetable juice only for the next five days.

Also take the following herbs daily:

- Ginger capsules - one with each meal (three capsules per day).

- Uva Ursi capsules - one in the morning and two in the evening

- Vitamin B6 - 250 mg

- Magnesium oxide - 300 mg

These supplements should be taken just before your meal to avoid burping. You do not need to duplicate the B6 and magnesium doses if you are already on them.

This herbal tea, as well as the parsley, can easily spoil. Reheat to boiling every third day if it is being stored in the refrigerator. Add HCl drops just before drinking. (If you sterilize it in the morning you may take it to work without refrigerating it in a glass container).

When you order your herbs, be careful; all herb companies are not the same. These roots should have a strong fragrance. If the ones you buy are barely fragrant, they have lost their active ingredients and you should switch to a different supplier. Only fresh roots can be used (excerpted from the book *The Cure for All Diseases* by Hulda Clark). An easier way to detoxify the kidneys might be the use of the uva ursi and juniper herbs in the form of supplements. Uva Ursi, also known as bearberry, has a specific affinity for the genito-urinary organs, especially for urinary tract infections, cystitis, nephritis, urethritis, hematuria (bloody urine), yeast infections, and vulvitis. Remember to increase your consumption of water while kidney cleansing.

~~***~~

Chapter Nine:
Cleanse Your Liver

Fatty Liver Disease and Liver Detoxification

More than ever before in the history of humankind, we need to have healthy livers to combat environmental toxins. If you talk to radiologists or gastroenterologists who are looking at people's liver today, they will tell you that the condition of *fatty liver* affects more than 50% of people over the age of fifty, and some much younger than fifty.

Most toxins, or poisons, reach our bloodstream when we swallow or inhale them. Others pass through our skin, while still others are released by dying cells or invading bacteria. Many of these toxins pass through the liver, the body's waste-purification plant, where they are broken down and removed from the blood before they can cause damage.

These susceptibilities to toxins are caused by poor diet, excessive alcohol intake, and adverse reactions to chemicals, pharmaceutical drugs, and or hepatitis. Gallbladder surgery is the most commonly performed operation in North America.

First, let me just say that if you have liver problems because of alcohol abuse, that it IS possible — I didn't say EASY — to change your behavior. We all know abusing alcohol is bad for us. Why do we do it then? Procrastination? Laziness? Mental barriers? Transcendental meditation has helped many people make marked improvements not only in their health and behavior, but also in various aspects of life. I highly recommend you look into it; it has favorably impacted all aspects of my life.

Facts:

Many things other than alcohol can cause liver and gallbladder problems. Every year, more than half a million people in the United States and more than 50,000 people in Canada, undergo surgery to remove their gallbladders because of gallstones.

- Ninety percent of people have gallstones to some degree.

- Eighty percent of people do not know that they have gallstones.

- Approximately 80% of all gallstones show no symptoms and may remain "silent" for years.

- More than 60 % of Americans will, in their lifetime, develop some of these health conditions: colitis, Crohn's disease, irritable bowel syndrome, allergies, arthritis and cancer.

Symptoms of liver disease include nausea, malaise, vomiting, fatigue, loss of appetite, itching, a yellow coloring of the skin or the eyes, pain in the right upper part of the belly and dark urine. The best way to determine whether your liver has been compromised is with some simple blood tests.

One of the best tools you can use to prevent gallstones is a simple liver cleansing procedure (Liver/Gallbladder Flush). This can be done in the comfort of your home and is very inexpensive, however, always try to be in the care of a health professional, i.e., a physician.

Be certain to complete the parasite and kidney cleanse program before beginning the following liver and gall bladder flush.

Liver and Gall bladder Flush Ingredients:

- 1/2 Cup Extra Virgin Olive Oil

- 1 Big grapefruit (or 2 small) or 3 lemons

- 4 tablespoon EPSOM salts

- 3 cups water

- 1/2 Cup Classic Coke (Optional - for taste only)

- One jar of Vitamin C powder

- 500 mg to 2 grams of L-Ornithine (L-*ornithine* is a basic amino acid and is important in the formation of urea.)

I recommend using grapefruit juice over lemon juice. The lemon juice sometimes doesn't mix with the oil as well as grapefruit juice. Begin the cleanse on Saturday so that you rest on Sunday.

Do not take any medication, vitamins, herbs or pills that you can do without during this flush; they could prevent success. Also stop the parasites and kidney program the day before starting the gall bladder/liver flush.

The morning before taking the flush, eat a no-fat breakfast and lunch such as cooked cereal with fruit, fruit juice (no butter or milk), baked potato or other vegetables with salt only. This allows the bile to build up and develop pressure in the liver. Higher pressure pushes out more stones.

Do not eat or drink after 2:00 p.m. If you eat after 2:00 p.m., you could feel quite ill later.

Get your Epsom salts ready. Mix 4 tbs. in 3 cups of water and pour this into a jar. You can substitute the 3 cups of water with 3 cups freshly juiced grapefruit-juice, or freshly pressed apple juice. This makes four servings, 3/4 cup each. Set the jar in the refrigerator to get ice cold (this is for convenience and taste only).

6:00 p.m.

Drink one serving (3/4 cup) of the ice cold Epsom salts. If you did not prepare this ahead of time, do it right now. You may also add 1/8 tsp. vitamin C powder to improve the taste. You may also drink a few mouthfuls of water afterwards or rinse your mouth. Get the Extra Virgin olive oil and grapefruit out to become room temperature.

8:00 p.m.

Repeat by drinking another 3/4 cup of Epsom salts. You haven't eaten since two o'clock, but you won't feel hungry. Begin your bedtime routine. The timing is critical for success; don't be more than 10 minutes early or late.

9:45 p.m.

Pour 1/2-cup (measured) extra virgin olive oil into the pint jar. Squeeze the grapefruit by hand into the measuring cup. Remove pulp with a fork. You should have at least 1/2 cup, more (up to 3/4 cup) is best. You may top it off with lemonade. Add this to the olive oil. Close the jar tightly with the lid and shake hard until watery (only fresh grapefruit does this).

Now visit the bathroom one or more times, even it makes you late for your ten o'clock drink. However, don't be more than fifteen minutes late.

10:00 p.m.

Drink the potion you have mixed. Take four ornithine capsules with the first sips to make sure you will sleep through the night. Take eight capsules of ornithine if you already suffer from insomnia. Take it to your bedside if you want, but drink it standing up. Get it down within 5 minutes (fifteen minutes for very elderly or weak persons).

Lie down IMMEDIATELY! You might fail to get stones out if you don't. The sooner you lie down the more stones you will get out. Be ready for bed ahead of time. As soon as the drink is down, walk to your bed and lie down flat on your back with your head up high on the pillow. Try to think about what is happening in the liver. Try to keep perfectly still for at least twenty minutes. You may feel a train of stones traveling along the bile ducts like marbles. There is no pain because the bile duct valves are open (thank you Epsom salts!). Go to sleep. You may fail to get stones out if you don't.

Next morning

Upon awakening, take your third dose of Epsom salts. If you have indigestion or nausea, wait until it is gone before drinking the Epsom salts. You may go back to bed. Don't take this potion before 6:00 AM.

2 hours later

Take your fourth (the last) dose of Epsom salts. Drink 3/4 cups of the mixture. You may go back to bed.

After 2 more hours you may eat. Start with fresh fruit juice. One-half hour later you should eat fruit. One hour later, you may eat regular food, but keep it light. By supper you should feel recovered.

How well did you do?

Expect diarrhea in the morning. Use a flashlight to look for gallstones in the toilet with the bowel movement. Look for the green kind since this is proof that they are genuine gallstones, not food residue. Only bile from the liver is pea green. The bowel movement sinks but gallstones float because of the cholesterol inside. Count them all roughly, whether tan or green. You will need to total 2,000 stones before the liver is clean enough to rid you of allergies or bursitis or upper back pains permanently. The first cleanse may rid you of them for a few days, but as the stones from the rear travel forward, they give you the same symptoms again. You may repeat cleanses at two-week intervals. Never cleanse when you are ill.

Sometimes, the bile ducts are full of cholesterol crystals that did not form into round stones. They appear as "chaff" floating on top of the toilet bowl water. It may be tan colored, harboring millions of tiny white crystals. Cleansing your body of this chaff is just as important as purging the stones.

How safe is the liver cleanse? It is very safe. My opinion is based on over five hundred cases of my own clients, including many persons in their seventies and eighties. None went to the hospital; none even reported pain, although it can make you feel quite ill for one or two days afterwards. In each of these cases of reported subsequent illness, the maintenance parasite program had been neglected. This is why the instructions direct you to complete the parasite and kidney rinse program first.

The truth is self-evident. People who have had their gallbladder removed surgically still get plenty of green, bile-coated stones, and anyone who cares to dissect their stones can see that the concentric circles and crystals of cholesterol exactly match textbook pictures of gallstones.

Detoxifying the Liver

Various nutrients are required in order for the liver detoxification to be carried out successfully. An adequate supply of these key antioxidants is essential to prevent further liver damage:

- 175 mg Milk thistle
- 2000 mg of Vitamin C (Ester C) is best.
- 200 mcg Selenium,

- 50 mg Beta carotine

- 400 mg of Vitamin E

- N-acetyl-cysteine (NCA are all powerful antioxidants which are helpful in liver detoxification.)

- Amino acid SAM-E (Plays an important role in liver health, in addition to helping with depression.)

- Cruciferous vegetables (Broccoli, cauliflower, brussels sprouts, cabbage, etc. have been shown to enhance liver detoxification. I use them regularly when vegetables juicing.)

- B vitamins as directed on bottle, including 100 mg of riboflavin and 15 mg niacin, also aid in liver detoxification.

Coffee Enema Helpful In Liver Detoxification

The coffee enema is used to detoxify the liver, not the colon. It is a low-volume enema that remains only in the sigmoid colon. There is a duct between the sigmoid colon and the liver called the *entero-hepatic circulation system*. When the stool reaches this point, it contains many toxins, which are sent to the liver for detoxification.

Without getting too technical here, the caffeine that is absorbed into the entero-hepatic system causes the liver ducts, including the bile ducts, to empty into the sigmoid colon. Releasing the toxins in the liver ducts makes room for toxins from the body to enter the liver for detoxification.

The alkaloids in the caffeine stimulate the production of an enzyme called *glutathione-S-transferase*, which is an enzyme that facilitates the liver detoxification pathways. The coffee enema is safe even for people who are sensitive to caffeine because the coffee remains in the sigmoid colon, where it will not be absorbed, provided the proper amount is used and the enema bag is not placed too high. If you are unsure of the placement, you can ask your hydro colon therapist to administer a coffee implant.

To further ensure the health of your liver, add the following supplements to your daily diet:

- Amylase (works to breakdown carbohydrates, i.e., starches, sugars)

- Bromelain (taken from pineapple plant; helps break down proteins)

- HCL hydrochloric acid (stimulates pancreatic secretion, activates pepsin, and sterilizes the stomach from bacteria and parasites)

- Lactase (works to break down lactose found in milk products)

- Lipase (works to break down fats into fatty acids and glycerol)

- Ox bile (improves fat digestion, stimulates bile flow, aids gallbladder)

- Pancreatin (contains protease, amylase, and lipase; functions in the intestine and in the blood)

- Papain (extracted from papaya fruit; aids in protein digestion)

- Pepsin (breaks down proteins; function depends on availability of hclprotease)

- Hcl protease (works to breakdown protein into amino)

~~***~~

Chapter Ten:
Start Walking, and Breathing More

Did you know that walking is one of the best exercises you can do to keep yourself healthy and in shape? If you walk just one mile a day you will burn at least 100 calories, and this could result in a loss of ten pounds in a year without changing your eating habits.

You don't need any special equipment or special training since you already know how to walk and breathe, and it's FREE. Of course, if you choose to use the facilities provided in a gym or other exercise emporium, you will have to pay. But why go around and around a track looking at the same old scenery — if there is any — when you can enjoy fresh air and take a different route every day by just taking a brisk stroll down the street?

The image that comes to mind when I think of "aerobics" is of a classroom setting with an instructor showing a lot of people how to make moves that seem almost like dancing. There's nothing wrong with that but you don't have to join an exercise group and invest in proper exercise attire to enjoy the benefits of aerobic exercise.

Aerobic exercise is defined as "conditioning the heart and lungs by increasing the efficient intake of oxygen by the body." Walking fits this description perfectly. But there are many more benefits that are realized by aerobic exercise.

Walking is a good way to condition the body for other more strenuous aerobic activities such as jogging. It also strengthens your leg and back muscles, improves the bones, strengthens the heart and gives one a sense of accomplishment that comes when you know you've done something good for yourself.

There is really no right or wrong way of walking, but for your own safety and comfort there are a few guidelines that you'll need to observe. You will of course, need to speak to a competent medical professional (your doctor) and get their approval before embarking on any exercise program, even walking. One of the most important aspects is to be sure you have proper shoes. No, you don't have to buy an expensive pair, but they should have cushioned heels, a flexible sole with wide toes, and a comfortable collar around the top edge. Wear clothing that allows you to move freely and is suitable for the weather or indoor environment.

As with any form of exercise, you should begin your session with warm-up and stretching exercises to prepare the muscles for activity and to prevent spasms or damage to the muscles. We're not talking about a professional warm-up here, just a few well-chosen exercises such as walking in place a few minutes, and stretching your leg and back muscles. It is suggested by some fitness experts that you gradually increase the speed and length of your steps regimen to receive maximum benefits by moving briskly until you achieve true stride. This means that the heart rate and pulse should reach a certain level, which is sustained for a period of time. For example, the rate to aim for is your target rate, beyond which there is no further health benefit. There are charts available to help you find your target rate, which is determined according to your age. You will have achieved aerobic benefits when you can keep up this rate for twenty minutes. Even if you don't get into monitoring your heart and pulse rate and walking at a sustained pace, the benefits you receive from walking for health are tremendous.

Thirty minutes of walking a day, at least five times a week, can improve muscle tone and strength. When you walk briskly on a regular schedule, you can:

- Improve your body's ability to consume oxygen during exertion

- Lower your resting heart rate

- Reduce blood pressure

- Increase the efficiency of your heart and lungs

Walking may also contribute to weight loss by burning calories, helping to maintain a good resting metabolic rate, and burning fat. To lose weight though, you might have to walk more than the minimum. Although results may vary with pace and speed, the President's Council on Physical Fitness and Sports reports that walking one mile can burn about 100 calories. Just fifteen minutes a day can translate to about ten pounds of weight loss per year.

What's more, there is little risk of injury from walking. But don't start or increase any exercise program — even walking — without first checking with your doctor.

Step by Step

Here are some tips to help you develop an efficient walking style:

- **Again start with simple warm-up exercises.** This includes putting your joints through easy ranges of motion.

- **Hold your head erect.** Keep your back straight and your abdomen flat. Point your toes straight ahead, and swing your arms loosely at your sides.

- **Land on the heel of your foot, then roll forward off the ball of your foot.** Walking only on the ball of the foot or in a flat-footed style may cause fatigue and soreness.

- **Take long, easy strides.** Lean forward slightly when walking on hills or at a very rapid pace.

- **Take deeper breaths as your pace quickens.** Breathe with your mouth open if that is more comfortable.

- **Take the "talk test" to help you find the right pace.** If you can't carry on a conversation while walking, you're going too fast.

- **When you're ready, increase the challenge.** Walk on hills, carry weights or increase your duration and speed, but do this as you gain experience.

Walking Gear

All you need is a proper pair of shoes, comfortable clothing, and some time. Whatever kind of shoe you select, it should have arch supports and a 1/2 to 3/4 inch heel. Choose a shoe with uppers made of materials that "breathe," such as leather or nylon mesh.

Consider getting a pedometer to track your steps. Start out slowly and keep an eye on your step log to figure out your average steps per day. Find ways to continue to add steps until you can reach 10,000 in one day.

Again, dress comfortably for weather conditions and wear layers. The extra layers help trap heat. When you start to warm up, you can shed your top layer and still feel comfortable. You also will want to bring along some water so you can keep drinking while you exercise.

I just looked out my window and saw an elderly couple in their seventies briskly walking down the street. Walking can accommodate mostly everyone; it doesn't matter whether you are old or young, stiff or flexible, in vibrant health, or recovering from a major trauma or illness. Whatever your condition, there is a pace and style of walking that will leave you feeling more refreshed and energized. Even an experienced runner with the ability to pound the pavement in a rousing roadside run can still find a cardiovascular challenge when combining good breathing techniques with walking. Walking while employing simple breathing techniques, such as exhaling twice as long as you inhale will help you to expel volatile toxins from the lungs. A prolonged exhalation emphasizes contraction of the abdominal muscles, thus activating the navel center, imparting additional heat and vitality. Observing the breath as you walk also clears the mind of mental chatter and self-talk. If you're thinking that that sounds like a formula for meditation-in-action, you're right. A brisk walk with breath awareness is mentally refreshing. It may leave you feeling as if you've just finished meditating rather than exercising vigorously.

The progression of attention from body to breath to energy and mind works while walking as well as in meditation; just keep the breath flowing and one foot on the ground.

~_***_~

Chapter Eleven:
Start Loving Your Own Life

Whose Life is This, Anyway?

It's time to define your own reality and create the life that will make you happy. This is your life, IT IS NOT A REHEARSAL. Create your own standard to measure your success. Many of us have been brainwashed into believing society's definition of success: lots of money, a high-powered job, a picture-perfect family, a big extravagant home, and a beautiful body. This might work for some people, but all too often we are left feeling dissatisfied, restless, sad and depressed. We can't all squeeze ourselves into the same mold, and we shouldn't want to. Take some time to figure out what you really want out of life and then develop a strategy to achieve it. Now let's begin with a few basic premises.

You Are a Unique, One of a Kind, Special Being. You Matter

No one else is more important, worthy, or special than you. A person is not more valuable because they are richer, more famous, more educated, or more attractive. There is goodness and love in you. Do not treat your own physical, emotional, and spiritual health as an afterthought. Make your own well being a priority. You deserve all the bounty this world has to offer. You are worth it.

Erase Negative Programming

Do away with all the old, negative messages you were given about yourself. If someone has told you that you are worthless, undeserving, dense or unattractive, that is their opinion and also their problem. No one has a right to judge you or belittle you. We are all struggling to get by in this world; and as much as I would like to think I have all of the answers, NO ONE HAS ALL THE ANSWERS. Honor your own truth. In your own heart, you know who you are; don't let another take that power away from you. Love yourself. Every once in a while I remind myself that I don't have to experience the world in the way I have been told.

Forgive Yourself … and Move On

Maybe like me, you did screw up, and were told that you were worthless as a person. Maybe you even were abused. Some of us have to learn the hard way. There are really no failures or mistakes, just opportunities for growth. Usually something good does come out of our mistakes or abuse. So learn from them, don't repeat them, and don't allow anyone to repeat the pattern, forgive them, forgive yourself, and move on.

Make Amends

If you've hurt someone else in the process of learning your life lessons, and most of us have, make it right. Reach out to them, and let them know how sorry you are. And if you are sorry, start being nice. You are accountable for your behavior. Own up to it.

Nurture Yourself

Life is full of peaks and valleys. Even though they are more difficult, you learn more during the valleys, i.e., the challenging times. When you are in a valley, you might not see the value of it, but in retrospect you will realize that you have learned a great deal. Know that nothing you experience is an accident. Everything you experience and everyone you meet teaches you something or holds a lesson for you. So be good to yourself. Be kind to yourself. Love yourself. If you are hurting, or sad or lonely, honor that. Make time for yourself. Let yourself heal. Don't expect so much of yourself. Life can be downright brutal. Let the love within you and others carry you through. In time, you will see how much you have learned. It is worth the journey.

All your life, you have been taught to invalidate your feelings. This is wrong. Your subconscious mind continually picks up and processes cues from your environment and from other people. This is valuable information that you should not disregard. Don't let a person talk you into doing something that doesn't feel right to you. Trust your gut. If something doesn't feel right to you, then it probably isn't. And you don't have to justify how you feel. Just say, "No thank you," or "I'd rather not," or "I'm busy." Everyone else does not know more than you.

When One Door Closes, Another Opens

Change is good. This is how you grow. Eventually you will see that sometimes you have to lose something to gain something else. Even illness, death, and financial loss have a purpose. Did a tragedy bring you closer to your family and friends?

Love Your Body

Your body houses your spirit and soul; it gets you what you need. Appreciate what your body can do and stop focusing on what it can't. No one else's body would be better for you. (Being thinner or better looking is not more valuable.) If you are not the most stunning person in town, then perhaps this makes you more approachable to others. Even if you have a physical disability, there is a reason for this. It is not to cause you to suffer, rather it is an opportunity for you to grow, or to understand, or to appreciate something in life. Perhaps this will be the vehicle through which you meet a kindred spirit or discover some hidden talent within you. Be at peace and trust that your soul is beautiful and so are you.

~~***~~

Chapter Twelve:
Bury Your Possessions Before Your Possessions Bury You

Healing the degenerative diseases of life takes a serious life-changing program. I have found that getting rid of one-third of all my possessions is one of the most powerful healing tools in my own life.

"Lay not up for yourselves treasures upon earth ..." Matthew 6:19

Do you know anyone who has ever won the rat race? Probably not. And yet, everywhere I go, I see men and women who are tired and worn out from trying to win this race that nobody wins.

We live in a world in which success is measured by the size of one's wealth or possessions, by one's accomplishments or fame, and in terms of one's IQ, GPA, educational degrees, talent, position or power.

Regrettably, this paradigm covers all categories of our society, and there is a temptation to view success in terms of these temporal realities. It is forgotten that fame, education, wealth, beauty, athletic prowess, talent, and power can easily be lost, but there are some things that are of enduring value such as compassion, love, generosity, kindness, sympathy, humility, etc. These virtues not only measure the greatness of a person, but they also reveal whom a person really is. We call these virtues *character traits*. These character traits are treasures in the health of all of us.

Ray Morgan, OM.D. Ph.D.

Some Probing Questions

If you were asked to list the five most important things in your life right now, what would they be?

When I posed that question to a group of people of different religious backgrounds at our **Insight for the Family, Inc.** Marriage and Singles Conference last year, their responses included their faith or religion, education, family, health, relationship, friends, job opportunities, and their reputation.

I'm sure most of us, especially young people, can identify with the above standard responses. But in an effort to probe a little further into what our conference attendees really valued in life, I asked them two follow-up questions:

• If you lived in a foreign country where a civil war suddenly erupted, what three possessions would you take with you if you had to leave right away?

• If your home were on fire, what items would you rescue before exiting?

To these questions, our attendees listed such items as their passports, Bibles, Koran, wallets, credit cards, computers, document files, old pictures, letters, and cell-phones.

I don't know what you would add to that list. Whatever you add, those items reveal the things you truly value in life. They are the things you hold dear and consider essential to your happiness, well being, survival, and security. They are your treasures, and your treasures determine your priorities. They reveal your true ambitions, your attractions, and your affections.

This is the decisive question: Are the things you presently treasure what they ought to be? Do your treasures have a lasting value? Will those treasures still be valuable in five or ten years? Would the value appreciate or depreciate? Would there come a time when you would lose interest in these things you presently hold dear? Do you see yourself ever giving them up, or exchanging them for something more valuable and enduring?

One way to ascertain what is of enduring value is to answer another

94

question I asked our attendees: "If your life were coming to an end today, what would be the things that you would mourn or regret losing?"

Unlike their responses to the previous questions, there was a very long pause before our attendees' volunteered answers to this particular question. Even then, the list was very insightful. They answered: "My life;" "My unconverted family members, friends, loved ones, and parents."

Now it should be clear from the last response that the most valuable things in life are neither of the tangible items listed above, but rather *eternal salvation* and that of others. If this is the case, then regardless of how successful you may be according to the world's standards, if in the conduct of your life you do not make choices that lead to eternal life, you are gambling away your most important treasure.

Facts:

- Your possessions take your attention and focus.

- Getting rid of one-third of what you own is akin to shock therapy, and gives you 33% more focus on the important things, such as healing yourself. It is a big wake-up call.

- Everyone has some possessions that actually are burdensome, rather than making life easier, more joyful, and contributing to their overall well being. Instead, these possessions add stress, make you sick and are killing you.

When someone has a degenerative disease, I view it as something they own that is making them sick and killing them. I have never seen an exception to this rule.

You will also see from my clients' case studies that getting rid of what are known as toxic possessions often create an emotional purge, creating huge leaps forward in physical healing.

In my clinic, I suggest to my clients that they bury their possessions before their possessions bury them. Possessions are not just things, but encompass whatever you covet. This can include wealth, accomplishments, fame, IQ, educational achievements, talent, physical appearance and clothing, or a particular circle of friends, a desire for attention, or longing for recognition. Other "possessions" include boyfriends and girlfriends, or some other special relationship. It also could be a position of power that distracts focus. Of course those things collected in homes or offices are included. Maybe it's all the "garbage" that you think are priceless relics, but you know is not. Or maybe it's all those broken parts stuffed in your garage that you think you might need someday, but never will.

After you are gone, your children will want to curse you for having to deal with all of your precious collections. They will probably end up selling it for $15.00 at a garage sale! Save them the time, trouble and emotional heartache and at the same time do yourself a healing favor, and get rid of all of it now. THROW IT AWAY.

What about the shoebox, the file box or drawer full of paper that you think is so important it can't be thrown away? You think it's important and you plan to sort through it one day? Trust me, you will never get to it but will stress yourself out thinking about it. Do yourself a gigantic favor. Walk the box to the nearest shredder. Shred them now and what you can't shred, throw away and scream, "Thank you LORD!"

Throwing away one-third of all the stuff you possess is powerful healing in itself. Remember, this stuff is not you, and it distracts you from living and will make you sick. Get rid of it.

I love to do house calls. Although they are a thing of the past, I advise all practitioners reading this book to conduct them. Usually I tell my clients I would like them to do ten visits to my office, with one visit scheduled every other week, so the entire program would take twenty weeks. In this period of time I give my clients a series of natural healing projects and programs to accomplish, like a health-building food program, a body detox, and a bowel cleansing program. By the end of the twenty weeks my clients feel much better than they have in weeks, if not their entire life. And of course, almost always their diseases and illnesses are gone. Whenever a client has a degenerative disease or a life-threatening illness, however, more than ten office visits are required. I also want to get to know them better. Like a great detective I probe for more facts, even the so-called trivial ones, to crack the case. So I make the third or forth visit a house call and go to the clients' home instead of them coming to my office. Often my clients would think this is a bit strange because it just isn't done these days. I make it very clear that my house call isn't an option; it is a necessity. When I arrive, I tell them that I would like to have a full tour of the house in its entirety.

They instantly get nervous. I often like to start with the living room, the bedroom and/or bathroom. I usually save the kitchen for last because I know that all the junk food has been thrown away in order to make a good impression. I am very good at what I do, I am a GREAT detective, so usually within the first 10 minutes I find IT; a possession so toxic that it is killing them.

Colitis Cured Instantly: Case Study #1.

Once I went on a house call to see a young woman at her apartment. She was twenty-two years old and had colitis so bad that she hadn't been to church in several weeks. Her pastor was worried so I checked in on her as a favor to her pastor. She was not a client of mine but knew of me and was expecting me. She had constant diarrhea-like bowel movements, about twenty a day, and was very sick. We talked for just a minute, and I then noticed her college graduation diploma hanging in an unusually prominent place- in the middle of her empty bedroom wall. She had graduated with honors at the very top of her class, something many people are proud of. When I remarked about it, I could immediately see that her whole body language changed. I asked her more and she began to get sick.

As it turned out she told me she absolutely hated college, every minute, every hour, every day, every week, every month, and every one of her college years. Her parents said that they would not continue to support her and would withdraw their financial support if she didn't go to college. She saw no choice. She went and hated every minute of it, yet she placed her degree on the most prominent place in the whole room.

I asked her if I could look at it closer. She looked a bit nervous but gave me permission to take it off the wall for closer inspection. I then asked whether I could look at it even closer by taking it out of the glass frame. Without hesitation she said "No". I explained to her that if I were going to be able to help her, I had to look at everything very closely. I think she thought that I was looking for some rare fungus or Legionnaire's Disease. Looking very nervous and uncertain, she acquiesced.

When I slipped her college magna cum laude degree out of the frame, I knew that I had struck gold. She started to cry and babble. *I love babble; that is when some of the most important information comes out.* She was actually having some dialogue with her parents saying that she'd told them how much she hated college and they refused to listen to her and had forced her to attend. She lost the sense that I was even in the room. I said, "Hey, look!" I tore her degree in half. Well, I got more physical shock out of her body than if I had double zapped her with a .44 caliber magnum. WOW, she flew back flat on her bed at first and then immediately shot forward just like the film of JFK when he was shot in Dallas. She immediately clutched her abdomen in pain, looked up at me sobbing and gasping just to see me rip the degree in half again. She vomited.

The long and short of this client and her colitis is that with a food program change, some intestinal cleansing, her colitis was gone in a few days, and never returned. The colitis irritant was an emotional flash back to the worst years of her life when her parents abandoned her. When she got rid of her emotional baggage she was able to heal her colitis.

Case Study #2

Mrs. Sandra Copeland (name changed to protect her privacy) was a fifty-seven year old woman with a malignant breast tumor. It was her first bout with cancer, but it was killing her. She had just completed her second round of chemotherapy and radiation and was told they could no longer help her. During this house call visit, as we were walking down the hall of her apartment after visiting her bedroom, I noticed we passed a room with a locked door. I asked her to open it, she said 'Oh no, I haven't opened that room in years." All the more reason to open it, I thought. I asked her to get the key, and after some resistance, she went and got the key. I knew I was on to something. When I finally got her to open the door it was like a children's museum frozen in time; it was spooky. There was children's furniture and toys and games everywhere. Much of them were covered with sheets. I asked her to tell me the story behind this room. With tears in her eyes she said, "This was my daughter's room. She died ten years ago." How old was she?" I asked. "Eight," she replied. It was noticeably painful for her to be in the room with me. I have heard it said that a parent should never have to bury a child and I totally understand that logic. Three years ago, I buried my oldest son, Scott. What a painful part of my life's journey! A parent is never prepared to deal with the death of their child. But I could see that this room was to her, her unburied child, a tomb, and she had to walk by it several times a day. I can imagine what grief, anger, sadness, and hell went through her mind and body every time she walked by the room. *I knew that the room had to go.*

As we sat down, I told her this room had to be dismantled, opened up, cleaned out, and the room turned into something new. She agreed, and asked, "What do I do with my daughter's possessions?" I suggested they be given to the good will. She began crying and looked at me as if I were out of my mind.

A woman's breasts are all about nurturing so in that moment I knew that she had to give, or throw, all the possessions away. She wanted to give them to her sister, but I said no. She had to get them out of her life. I was quite convincing. After all it was a matter of life and death. I asked her to carry them by herself out to the hallway for the good will. She was sobbing hysterically, drooling, and gagging. On her second trip she had a pain so sharp in her breast that it caused her to double over. She said, "It was the worst pain I have ever had." After a while she continued removing the items. It took most of the day, and when she finished she collapsed at the door.

It turned out that getting rid of her daughter's possessions was the absolute turning point for Mrs. Copeland. She went on to bury her daughter emotionally and also to heal her breast cancer. It's been six years. I have talked to her from time to time. She is on a nutritional program and the cancer has not returned.

Many of my case histories often reveal that people who develop cancer almost always had some horrible experience in the previous two years before the cancer surfaced, an experience they could not deal with.

Getting rid of accumulated toxic waste in your life is as healing as getting rid of toxic waste in your body.

~~***~~

Chapter Thirteen:
Hot and Cold Hydrotherapy
(Water Therapy)

What? Hydrotherapy? YES, HOT AND COLD WATER

Hydrotherapy is the use of water in the treatment of disease. *Hydrothermal therapy* additionally uses its temperature effects, as in hot baths, saunas, wraps, etc.

Historical Perspective

Hydro- and hydrothermal therapies are traditional methods that have been used for the treatment of disease and injury by many cultures and has been around for centuries. The ancient Egyptians took therapeutic baths. Water is an important ingredient in the traditional Chinese and Native American healing systems. Therapeutic use of water was used in the 19th century. There are now many dozens of methods of applying hydrotherapy, including baths, saunas, douches, wraps, and packs.

Hydrotherapy is the application of water to initiate cure. All three forms of water (liquid, steam, and ice) can be used therapeutically. Advantages to hydrotherapy are:

- It is almost always available.

- It is easy to learn and perform.

- It is painless and has no ill side effects.

- It is inexpensive and can be done at home.

The goal of hydrotherapy is to improve the circulation and quality of blood. This is important because blood delivers nutrients to, and removes wastes from, tissues and organs. If circulation is poor or slow, healing nutrients cannot be delivered and toxins cannot be removed, which causes degeneration of the tissues and organs. By improving the quality of blood flow, more nutrients are available for cells to use and toxins are managed more efficiently.

General therapeutic uses of hydrotherapy include:

- Reduction in pain and swelling of injuries
- Reduction of fever
- Elimination of toxins
- Antispasmodic
- Alleviation of constipation
- Improvement of immune function

Alternating hot and cold (*contrast hydrotherapy*) is a common hydrotherapy treatment. The hot application expands blood vessels, filling them with blood, and the cold application constricts the blood vessels, forcing the blood to move on to other parts of the body. Hot and cold can be applied to any part of the body that is inflamed, congested, or injured. Treatment normally consists of applying a hot cloth for 3 minutes then a cold cloth for 30 seconds, alternating 3 times in a row.

The treatment can be done several times a day. The amount of time the hot and cold is applied may vary (e.g., 5 minutes hot, 1 minute cold) as long as the cold application is of shorter duration than the hot. It is also important to end the treatment with the cold application. The hot application should be pleasantly hot. **Caution:** Do not apply water that is hot enough to burn. People have different tolerance levels for hot water on different parts of their body. Tolerance levels can change from treatment to treatment, depending on emotional state, degree of injury or illness, and body temperature.

Water works on the body reflexively. This means that when water is applied to one part of the body, other parts of the body are also stimulated by an arterial (blood vessel) reflex or spinal cord reflex. Hydrotherapy takes advantage of this reflexive action. For example, if the left foot is fractured and in a cast, an alternating hot and cold treatment can be performed on the right foot. Because of the reflexive action, the left foot obtains the benefits of the hydrotherapy treatment even though it was done on the right foot. This principle is also used when a hot and cold treatment is applied to the feet to treat the throat or sinuses.

Hydrotherapy treatments include the following:

Baths and showers

Baths and showers can be healthy and healing. A hot bath or shower can encourage relaxation, reduce stress, and flush out toxins. Adding essential oils or herbs to the bath can enhance the therapeutic benefits. Cold baths and showers can be energizing and stimulating. A rinse of cold water after a hot shower can invigorate, boost the immune system, and improve blood flow.

Hot Foot Bath

A hot foot bath is the immersion of both feet and ankles in hot water for 10–30 minutes. It is an excellent way to draw blood from inflamed or congested areas of the body. Indications for use are foot and leg cramps, sore throat, cold, flu, nausea, insomnia, and chest or pelvic congestion.

Cold Rubbing

Soak a white linen cloth in cold water, wring out the water from the linen and briskly rub the entire body. Then go to bed until the body is warm and dry. This is for invigoration of the body. It tones up the body and promotes blood flow, and it is tremendous for problems of circulation or infections of the respiratory system.

Douches

Douches are not only for the vagina, but also for various parts of the body. Gentle douches can be applied with a watering can or hose. The water should not splash, but gently envelop the skin. The water stream should always be directed from the periphery toward the heart. After douching, stroke off excess water with your hand, dress, and exercise. There are various types of douche:

- **Knee douche.** The water stream is directed from the right small toe, along the outside of the lower leg to the hollow of the knee, then back along the inside and over the sole of the foot. The process is then repeated for the left leg. It is useful for headaches and migraines, low blood pressure, sleeplessness, contusions, and varicose veins. This treatment influences the digestive and reproductive organs and can help ward off vascular damage. Do not use for urinary tract infections, irritable bladder, sciatica, or during menstruation.

- **Thigh douche.** This is the same as the procedure for a knee douche, but includes the upper thigh. It can stimulate blood flow and help improve poor circulation. Useful for the treatment of *v*aricose veins, muscular rheumatism, crural paralysis, coxarthritis. Do not use for urinary tract infection, irritable bladder, sciatica, or during menstruation.

- **Lower trunk douche.** This is the same as the procedure for the thigh douche, but includes the lower trunk. It is useful for diabetes mellitus, meteorism, enlargement of the liver, and enlargement of the gallbladder and stone formation. Do not use for urinary tract infections, irritable bladder, sciatica, or during menstruation.

- **Arm douche.** Direct the water stream from the outside of the right hand to the shoulder, and then back on the inside of the arm. Repeat the process for the left arm. This is useful for cold hands, nervous disorders, neuralgia and paralysis, rheumatism of the arms, heart problems, vertigo, headaches, catarrh in the nose and throat.

- **Chest douche.** Douche the arms first. This is useful for chronic bronchitis, bronchial asthma, and angina pectoris. **Caution:** Moderate the temperature if there is risk of angiospasm. *Angiospasm* is spasmodic contraction of the blood vessels with increase in blood pressure. When doing this procedure be sure to be in the care of a health care professional.

- **Upper trunk douche.** This involves the upper torso and arms. It can be used to improve blood flow to the lungs, heart, and pleura. It's also useful for the treatment of bronchitis, bronchial asthma, disease of the larynx and vocal cords, headaches, nervous excitability, varicose veins of the legs, for toning-up, and for stimulating cardiac and respiratory activity. *Caution:* Do not use if there is blood stasis in the pulmonary circulation, or if you are having problems with high blood pressure. The term blood stasis refers to the path in which the blood circulates resulting in blocked or poor circulation.

- **Back douche.** Useful for the treatment of weakened back muscles, back pain, spinal disease, multiple sclerosis, bronchial asthma, nearly all diseases of the lung. *Warning:* Do not use in debilitated patients or those with neurasthenia.

- **Neck douche.** Useful for headaches, migraines, tenseness in the shoulder and neck, hypersensitivity to changes in the weather, mild depression, tinnitus, vertigo, arthritis of the hand and finger joints. *Warning:* Not to be used in persons with high blood pressure, enlargement of the thyroid, or raised intraocular pressure.

- **Face douche.** Proceed from the right temple downward to the chin, upward to the left temple, from right to left over the forehead, and repeatedly from the forehead to the chin, then in circles over the face. This is useful for relieving headaches and migraines, trigeminal neuralgia, toothaches, and for relaxing tired eyes. *Caution:* Keep the eyes closed.

Sauna and Steam Baths

Saunas and steam baths are similar in effect; the decision to take one rather than the other will be guided by personal preference. In a sauna, the heat acts more quickly to eliminate toxins through the skin, though some consider the moist air of a steam bath to have a more satisfying effect on the respiratory system. Saunas are deeply relaxing and are a great way to melt away stress.

A sauna is an eliminative procedure; it stimulates blood flow, increases the heart rate, has an immune-modulating effect, promotes hormone production, encourages mucosal secretions in the respiratory system, opens the airways, reduces resistance to respiration, regulates and relaxes the vegetative system, and can improve mental outlook. Children can start to take saunas at two or three years of age.

Chapter Fourteen:
Wear Cotton and Other
Natural Fibers

Natural fabrics come to the aid of the time-pressed consumer. Ask any woman what she would love to have more of these days and most would answer time and money.

With more and more demands on women, today's wardrobes have to perform like never before. Clothes have to be comfortable, go from desk to dinner and weekend wear, be well priced, and of course, be easy to maintain. Easy-care fabrics satisfy the many requirements today's shoppers have when looking for clothes. While the notion of washable fabrics is not new to some, it is one that is catching on quickly with designers as well as with scores of shoppers. According to Cotton Incorporated's Lifestyle Monitor™, 40% of women believe the cleaning instructions are very important when purchasing a garment. This compares to 32% who think the instructions are somewhat important, and 27% who think it is not at all important.

Bridge Clothing designer Eileen Fisher believes in the all-natural, easy-care fabric route so much, she practically founded her company on that premise back in 1984. The designer, whose customer is age 35-50, has had washable fabrics in her line every season since her first, and now uses them for both career and weekend dress. "We are constantly working toward the goal of making all of the fabrics we run completely washable," says Fisher. Her arsenal of washables includes a lot of cotton and washable wool crepe, which is both seasonless and versatile, because of what she calls "packability." "It just doesn't wrinkle," she says. Ditto for her washable silk crepe which Fisher says steams out in a snap. The designer has even had washable cotton velvets in her line.

Apparently natural fabrics represent a certain sense of quality to the consumer as well. In fact, Monitor results show that 68% of all those polled agree that better quality garments are made with natural fabrics. Of course, the idea of washable fabrics was one that retailers may not have embraced at first. No matter, though, consumers embraced washable fabrics almost immediately. "We borrowed the idea of washable fabrics from men's wear, thinking it was an option for women," says Karen Q. Micciulla, vice president of group development and director of Liz Claiborne Casual. "The stores agreed to test it back in 1996, but were not excited about it at first," she says. "The customer responded unbelievably well the moment it hit the floors, and the concept has continued to grow and evolve ever since." Claiborne's easy-care clothing lines include cotton twills, linens, linen and cotton blends, yarn-dyed shirting, and cotton and Lycra twill for everything from dresses, big shirts, drawstring skirts and pants. "We originally started using easy-care fabrics to make classic silhouettes such as pleated trousers," says Micciulla, "but wherever we have offered it, the customer has responded favorably. Spring and summer are stronger for us in terms of the amount of easy-care fabrics we offer."

Micciulla says Claiborne's fabrics cater to both the career woman and the weekend "warriorette." "We are finding out that it is more about lifestyle," says Micciulla. "A woman wants to be comfortable and have easy-care to wear for work and on the weekend. Anything we can do to make dressing easier seems to help."

L.L. Bean, the Freeport, Maine-based catalogue company which has specialized in weekend dressing for years, made the foray into career clothes last January with the launch of Freeport Studio, a label devoted entirely to the active, busy working woman.

"We, the developers at Freeport Studio, asked ourselves, what problem does this particular item solve," says Fran Philip, senior vice president and general manager of Freeport Studio.

"Clothing should be easy to wear and especially easy to care for," she says, adding that 80% of the spring and summer line is machine washable.

Philip says easy-care fabrics used in the Freeport Studio collections run the gamut - everything from washable linen, to wool, rayon, cotton, polyester, and silk for silhouette-dresses, pants, jackets, tops, and sweaters. Wool, cotton, linens and rayon, however, are the staple of the studio, because of the ease of care, loose fit, comfort, and easy style. She went on to say: "Most of our bodies are more loose fitting for a relaxed, comfortable, and easy style, versus traditional business wear such as tailored suits and dresses which are dry clean only," says Philip. "The response we have been getting from our customers has been very positive. Most have asked us, "What took you so long?"

While Philip's says Freeport Studio will expand the line each season, they will continue to ask the problem-solving questions when developing an item. "An expensive suede coat that is dry clean only will not be in our line. It does not solve a problem."

Many jock itch and vaginal infections, which include symptoms of itching, odor, and discharge, may decrease just by wearing cotton underwear. Cotton helps to keep the vagina free of excessive moisture, and allows the area to "breathe". Many women turn to different materials due to their clothing design or cut, but cotton underwear now comes in many shapes and sizes. The benefit of cotton underwear makes it a comfortable and healthy choice for the many men and women who wear them. Ventilating the vagina can also prevent the buildup of moisture and odor causing bacteria. Cotton absorbs excess moisture and removes build up heat from the area. Cotton is one of the only materials that become stronger when wet and is easily sterilized after use. It is especially important to wear cotton underwear throughout the summer or during times of high humidity. This is the best time for yeast infections, itching, and odor to occur. Avoid underwear at night entirely if cotton is not available. Using cotton underwear or eliminating underwear will keep the area dry throughout the night.

Cotton is by far one of the most absorbent textiles ever produced. It can hold many times its weight in water. In fact, it is used in the fabrication of not only clothes, but also other products that are used to absorb liquid, more so than any other material. It is the fibers that make up cotton that causes it to absorb water. Natural fabrics tend to be much more absorbent and more comfortable than synthetic fabrics. The looseness of the fibers of the natural fabric also allow for it to be more breathable, making it a better choice for your skin. Cotton is much more absorbent than many other fabrics because of its molecular structure. The arrangement of the molecules in cotton creates an abundance of places to which water can be attracted. Other fabrics, especially synthetic ones, have fewer places for water molecules to bond, therefore, even though other fabrics will attract and hold some water, they do not have the capacity to absorb like cotton fibers. Most people don't realize that synthetic fabrics are teeming with chemicals and dyes that cannot be washed out, making them a potential health hazard.

Toxins in Your Textiles

Most synthetic fabrics, from towels to dress shirts to bed linens, are treated with chemicals during and after processing. These chemicals not only leach into the environment, leaving an impact on groundwater, wildlife, air and soil, but they also may be absorbed or inhaled directly.

> "The use of man-made chemicals is increasing, and at the same time we have warning signals that a variety of wildlife and human health problems are becoming more prevalent," says Dr. Richard Dixon, Head of the World Wildlife Federation (WWF) in Scotland. "It is reckless to suggest there is no link between the two and give chemicals the benefit of the doubt. Urgent action is needed to replace hazardous chemicals with safer alternatives especially in clothing and other consumer products."

WWF is so concerned about one fairly new clothing additive that, in 2004, they advised parents to check their children's clothing labels. If the chemical is on it, they advise switching to clothing made from natural fibers whenever possible.

Teflon in Your Trousers

The chemicals that the WWF was warning about are *per fluorinated chemicals* (PFCs), which include the non-stick additive Teflon. These chemicals are increasingly being added to clothing because it makes them last longer and also can make them wrinkle-free. Most clothing labeled "no-iron" contains PFCs.

What's the problem with PFCs? They are very toxic to the human body.

The U.S. Environmental Protection Agency (EPA) says that PFCs are cancer-causing compounds. However, "no-iron" and "wrinkle-free" pants have become a popular part of many schools' compulsory uniforms. Hardly the thing you'd like to send your child off to school in, but other options usually aren't provided.

"Without knowing it, parents are exposing their children to toxic chemicals in clothing that could have serious future consequences for their health and the environment. Children are usually more vulnerable to the effects of chemicals than adults, so the presence of these substances in school clothing is particularly alarming,' says Dr. Dixon.

Choosing organic clothing is beneficial for the environment because it is the eco-friendly alternative to synthetic clothing. Wearing organic clothing is beneficial for the individual because the clothing is natural, non-toxic, and practical. Purchasing organic is actively supporting the use of a sustainable material. When dollars are directed towards green practices, such as growing hemp and cotton, they are spent not only to receive a desired product, but also to encourage more eco-friendly work. When money supports irresponsible production practices, those actions will inevitably continue.

~~***~~

Chapter Fifteen:
Have More Sex

Sex isn't just good; it's good for you. Okay, I realize you probably think there is some wishful thinking going on because I'm a man. I personally have no evidence to prove my case, and the science isn't exact, but evidence is accumulating that the more sex you have, the better off you are. Without sex there would be no life.

. Over ten million American women are infertile.

. Nine million women use medical infertility services, Women often spend an average of more than $50,000 on infertility treatments or as much as $50,000 to secure donor eggs in order to have children according to Extend Fertility, Inc. Woburn, Massachusetts

. Medical infertility services have an 87% failure rate.

. Five hundred thousand American women will have their ovaries and uterus cut out this year.

. Over 65% of American men in their forties have prostate disease and 15 million men have prostate tumors.

. Fifty-five percent of all American men have some degree of erectile dysfunction and impotence.

. American males' sperm count has dropped to half of what it was only 70 years ago

. Viagra sales top 2 billion dollars in spite of dangerous, even lethal side effects.

. Ten percent of all American men can't even get an erection.

There is one caveat, though. "We do not have good data to show a direct connection to all-around good health," says Jennifer Bass, the head of information services at the Kinsey Institute for Research in Sex, Gender and Reproduction in Bloomington, Indiana. "We know that healthier people have more sexual activity. But we do not know which comes first. Does the good health make you more willing to have sex, or does the sex have a positive impact?"

Men and women who have a very strong sexual drive should know that the assumed health benefits of sex are generally thought to accrue to people in loving, monogamous relationships or those flying solo. Risky sex with lots of partners will probably do more harm than good.

But while researchers try to nail down the impact of sexual activity on overall health, data is mounting when it comes to some specifics. Here are several potential benefits:

1. Easing depression and stress

The release from orgasm does much to calm people. It helps us with sleep and stress whether or not we are having solo sex or sex with a partner.

A recent study of college students at the State University of New York in Albany suggests that semen acts as an antidepressant. Females in the study who were having sex without condoms (see safe sex caution above) had fewer signs of depression than women who used condoms or abstained from sex.

"These data are consistent with the possibility that semen may antagonize depressive symptoms," the authors wrote, "and evidence which shows that the vagina absorbs a number of components of semen that can be detected in the bloodstream within a few hours of administration."

Believe it or not, semen is good nutrition. It gives a shot of zinc, calcium, potassium, fructose and proteins; it's a veritable cornucopia of vitality. It is as good as breakfast, with freshly juiced oranges! (sorry I got carried away a bit.)

2. Orgasm as a pain reliever

Orgasm is a powerful painkiller. There is a natural chemical in the body called oxytocin. Just before and during a climax, the body releases this natural painkiller, along with a couple of other compounds like endorphins.

According to a study by Beverly Whipple, professor emeritus at Rutgers University and a famed sexologist and author, when women masturbated to orgasm "the pain tolerance threshold and pain detection threshold increased significantly by 74.6% and 106.7% respectively."

3. A cardiovascular booster

The semen in itself has the ability to lower the blood pressure of a woman. A recent study found that women who gave their men oral sex, and swallowed his sperm, had a lower risk of preeclampsia, the dangerously high blood pressure that sometimes accompanies pregnancy.

"The present study shows that oral sex and swallowing sperm is correlated with a diminished occurrence of preeclampsia," say the Dutch authors Jelle M. Schaaf.

There have been other studies showing that sex lowers blood pressure, and might even protect against stroke because of its stress-relieving ability. On the other hand, I remember hearing about former New York Governor Nelson Rockefeller who had a heart attack during a sexual encounter. Well, during the encounter it is natural for the blood pressure to rise. Without a rise in blood pressure an erection is not possible. The blood pressure should return to normal shortly thereafter; that is why men become so relaxed that they fall asleep.

What happened to Governor Rockefeller is not a regular occurrence, so enjoy this very important part of life, because sex does actually protect the heart. A 2002 report of a large population of British men said, "some protection from fatal coronary events may be an added bonus" of frequent sexual intercourse.

4. Countering prostate disease:

Over the past few years, several journals have published studies showing that the more ejaculations a man have, the better the health of the prostate.

Now the Journal of the American Medical Association no less, has reported "high ejaculation frequency was related to decreased risk of total prostate cancer." It doesn't matter how a man climaxes -- intercourse or masturbation. So next time he says, "Really, honey, it's therapy," he could be telling the truth.

When the body is weak, toxic and sick, sperm count goes down. Today, due to modern living, American males have half the sperm count we had seventy years ago. Also when you are not healthy, your hormone level goes down, your circulation gets clogged and you can lose your ability to get an erect penis. Nature's response to sickness and disease is the loss of our reproductive ability because nature resists and sometimes refuses to allow the procreation of sickness and disease. I realize that some of you men reading this believe that you are reasonably healthy. Well, think again. What most people think of as "good health," really is just a state of managed disease. Losing your ability to procreate, your potency, is a grave sign of bad health.

Although the above refers to men, quite a bit of it applies to women's health as well. When you are weak, toxic and sick, your hormone levels become imbalanced. You may stop ovulating, which means there is no release of eggs for fertilization. Even if you ovulate, your uterus may be toxic and infected and may not be able to hold or feed the fetus. Also when you are weak, sick, diseased, unhealthy, obese, anorexic, stressed out, and crazy, a woman's body has a natural intuitive survival mechanism. It protects you during this time from any additional physical or emotional stress, which could kill you (such as carrying a child for nine months). One of the most basic functions of the human body is survival, so temporary sterilization is your body's way of protecting you from killing yourself. If the woman happens to get pregnant, she usually spontaneously aborts the fetus.

5. Healing wounds

Some evidence suggests sex can be rejuvenating to the point of helping wounds to heal faster. Several experiments have shown that oxytocin can help even stubborn sores (like those suffered by diabetics) to heal by regenerating certain cells.

6. Fighting aging

Maybe it's the rejuvenation, maybe the happiness, maybe all of the above. One thing is for sure: "Use it or lose it" is literally true. For example, postmenopausal women often suffer from "vaginal atrophy," which is what it sounds like and can lead to all sorts of complications like urinary tract infections. What is one way to prevent it? More intercourse. Sex is a form of exercise, after all, and like all exercise, it burns calories and can help battle the onslaught of the years. In fact, nursing home experts say they wish oldsters would have more sex. Can sex really make you live longer? Perhaps. In the same population of British men I cited earlier, researchers found a 50 percent reduction in overall mortality in the group of men who said they had the most orgasms. There was a dose response: the more orgasms, the better.

Of course, as Kinsey's Bass reminds us, it could be that these blokes were just healthier and felt like having sex more often. But since there's no evidence that lots of sex is bad for you, what have you got to lose? Kinsey Institute for Sexuality Studies. Be sure your partner is healthy!!!

~~***~~

Chapter Sixteen:
Listen to Jokes and Laugh More

A good chuckle doesn't just cheer you up, but, doctors are discovering, it can ease pain and even help fight disease. Go on and have a giggle, or better yet, have a belly laugh.

"A cheerful heart is a good medicine, but a downcast spirit dries up the bones." Proverbs 17:22

The original Hebrew definitions:

merry = blithe, gleeful, be glad, joyful, making merry

medicine = a cure

It is said that laughter lifts our spirits. That might be so, I know life becomes worth living. Try it. You'll experience that vanishing state of being called relaxation. You will stress less and enjoy the company of other people more. When you laugh you become fully present in the moment.

"Life is too important to be taken seriously." Oscar Wilde

We are a nation of serious people who have serious health problems, many of which are related to stress. Laughter relieves stress. Through laughter we cope with our fear and anger, the two emotions, which result in stress.

Doctors and health care workers are finding that laughter may indeed be the best medicine. Laughing removes stress hormones and boosts immune function by raising levels of disease-fighting proteins called *gamma-interferon*, and *T-cells*, which produce disease-destroying antibodies. Laughter also triggers the release of endorphins, the body's natural painkillers, and produces a general sense of well being. Hospitals are incorporating laughter therapy programs into their therapeutic recommendations. The threshold of pain is raised during, and for a short period of time after, an episode of laughter.

Laughter engages various parts of the brain. Peter Derks from the College of William and Mary in Williamsburg, Virginia showed that humor pulls the various parts of the brain together rather than activating a component in only one area. Perhaps this is one reason why people often find that a dose of lengthy laughter can be followed by a burst of creativity and group problem solving. Laughter is also a good cardiovascular workout. It increases the activity of the heart and stimulates circulation. In addition, after the laughter subsides, the cardiovascular system goes into a state of relaxation. Researchers recorded what they call "mirthful laughter" and found that levels of interleukin 6, a cytokine that plays a central role in inflammation, dropped significantly in arthritis patients, but not in a healthy comparison group. The anti-inflammatory effects have also been shown to last for 12 or more hours after the laughter has subsided.

Pain can be eased by laughter too. When researchers at the University of California exposed children between the ages of seven and sixteen years to a pain experiment, where they put their hands into very cold water, those who watched a funny video and laughed were able to tolerate more pain.

Laughter is strong medicine for mind and body

Laughter is a powerful antidote to stress, pain, and conflict. Nothing works faster or more dependably to bring your mind and body back into balance than a good laugh. Humor lightens your burdens, inspires hopes, connects you to others, and keeps you grounded, focused, and alert. With so much power to heal and renew, the ability to laugh easily and frequently is a tremendous resource for surmounting problems, enhancing your relationships, and supporting both physical and emotional health.

Social Benefits of Laughter

Laughter connects us with others. Laughter is contagious, so by laughing you most likely will help others around you to laugh more and realize these benefits, too. By elevating the mood of those around you, you can reduce their stress levels, and perhaps improve the quality of social interaction you experience with them, thus reducing your stress level even more.

Find Humor In Your Life

Instead of complaining about life's frustrations, try to laugh about them. If something is so frustrating or depressing it's ridiculous, realize that you could "look back on it and laugh." Think of how it will sound as a story you could tell to your friends, and then see if you can laugh about it now. With this attitude, you may also find yourself being more lighthearted and silly, giving yourself and those around you more to laugh about. Approach life in a more mirthful way, and you'll find you're less stressed about negative events. You will achieve the health benefits of laughter.

Fake It Until You Make It

Just as studies show the positive effects of smiling occur whether the smile is fake or real, faked laughter also provides the benefits mentioned above. So smile more and fake laughter; you'll still achieve positive effects, and the fake merriment may lead to real smiles and laughter.

Don't sweat the small stuff. Guess what — it is all small stuff.

Chapter Seventeen:
Listen To Your Inner Voice

Your inner voice is trying to help you. Do you listen? Really listen?

Create some quiet time every day. Take time to breathe, to meditate, and to practice listening to your inner voice. When you hear that "little voice" talking to you, please...listen to it.

There is much more to life here on earth than what you can see and what you can actually touch and put your finger on. I always talk about what you feel in your guts, in your heart, in your soul, and about following the voice of God that is within you, that is within all of us. So have some quiet time every day. Some time to breathe, to meditate and listen.

You definitely need to start looking within yourself for answers if you find that you're constantly feeling confused and anxious.

Did you know that your outer voice could be a good starting point to begin providing those answers? Keep in mind that the words you express and your overall attitude are a direct extension of the thoughts you allow to fill up your mind. You can begin to dig deeper as soon as you really understand how your thoughts relate to your emotional state and what manifests in your life.

When you dig deeper within yourself, you begin to hear your inner voice. Your inner voice is much deeper than the thoughts of the mind. It's more spiritual in nature. Think of it as your life's guidance system.

Sometimes you'll find that this inner voice communicates to you in a subtle way where you just have a "feeling". Maybe it's to remember a birthday or that little reminder to call a good friend.

It can be a much louder signal at other times. You may feel a nagging feeling that there's something in your life begging for your attention. This could be why you're having those anxious feelings. Many people stay in this state of confusion and never take time to sit and start to really figure out what these inner feelings are trying to say. Don't fall into this same trap.

Now, it's time to go to another level with this. I want you to ask yourself whether you're seeing your life from your ego's outlook or from the perspective of your spiritual soul. When you think from an ego's viewpoint, you'll find you make decisions that create turmoil. Your spiritual self makes your ego insignificant. Therefore, your ego is afraid of your spiritual self and does everything possible to make you feel insecure and inadequate.

Your inner voice lets you know that you're OK just the way you are. It's OK to accept yourself as you are and then work on improving yourself in a healthy way. You'll know when your spiritual self is guiding you. It's when you experience feelings of inner peace and abundance. Pay attention to these moments. Really listen. Your inner voice will offer its own words of spiritual encouragement to you. Your spirit allows your inner soul to tell you what you need in order to avoid all the inner turmoil.

How to Live in Peace with Yourself

As soon as you decide to live in peace with yourself, your ego tries to step in and negate everything your spiritually-inclined inner voice is trying to help you understand.

- The ego is talking when you think you don't measure up or are worthless.

- It's talking when it's telling you that you have to constantly be on the go.

- It tells you that there is no time to reflect and understand the spiritual you.

Your ego wants you to live a hurried life wherein you multi-task and have a trillion things going at once, so the ego is not threatened by spiritual thoughts of inner peace and abundance. But you know that inside there's this tiny little voice you push away. Your inner voice whispers to you that this rushed lifestyle isn't what makes you feel fulfilled inside. If you keep ignoring it, you'll become more miserable over time.

Take the effort to put aside time to be alone without interruption. It could be time spent in prayer, in meditation, or just quiet time. It could be going for a walk. I get in touch with my inner voice sometimes when I go running. When I run it's just me with my inner thoughts and the world around me.

Find whatever works for you. Your inner voice will enlighten you on what you need in order to feel inner peace and abundance if you allow it to. Quiet your mind and listen. It's possible to experience inner peace and still live a productive, prosperous life. It's a choice you make.

Change Your Life

Call it "God," call it the "Holy Spirit," call it ancestor's guidance," or call it an "inner voice." Call it your "guardian angel." Call it whatever you want. I'm referring to that little voice that seems to talk to you now and then. We have all had an experience where "something" has told us about an impending event that was about to impact upon our lives. I have, and it made a difference.

There have been several occasions in which my guardian angel "spoke" to me. Permit me to share with you my most memorable example that occurred a few years ago. Believe it or not, this is a true story.

When my youngest son was four years old, one evening my wife put him to bed at 8:30 p.m. as she did every night. She and I went to bed at 11:00 p.m. At 2:00 a.m., while still asleep, a still voice spoke to me saying, "Wake up and check on your son." I ignored it and fell back asleep. One hour later the inner voice spoke to me again saying, "Wake up and check on your son." One-half hour later I heard the same admonition from my inner voice and that time, I got up. I checked on my son and found that he had a temperature of 102 degrees and was unresponsive. I got his temperature down then called his homeopathic pediatrician. My wife and I rushed him to his pediatrician's office. The doctor said if we had not acted as quickly as we did, our son would have died. Was this a random incident? Based on my experience with the inner voice, I don't think so. I do believe, however, someone or something alerted me to the danger my son was in that night. Was it my guardian angel? Was God speaking to me? I do not know.

What better way of creating a more fulfilling life than by mastering the art of tuning into your most inspired and ingenious self? Your inner voice is your guide of all guides to a life of greatness. You cannot attune to this inspiring voice without living a more inspiring life. Genius, creativity, and a silent power emerge from your heart and mind the moment you do. The secret of tuning in to its magnificent messages is having a heart filled with gratitude. When your heart is opened wide with gratitude, your inner voice becomes loud and clear, and your most life-expanding messages enter into your mind with ease. If your heart is filled with gratitude, it is almost impossible to stop your inner voice from speaking clearly and profoundly. Many great spiritual revelations and mental attributes are suddenly birthed from within you when your voice on the inside becomes louder than the many voices or opinions on the outside.

The great masters of life have been those who have mastered the ability to tune in to their great inner voices. Those great beings that mastered this talent left their marks in history. From Jesus Christ, who listened to his heavenly Father, to Dante, who listened to Beatrice, to Martin Luther King, Jr., Malcolm X, R. Buckminster Fuller and many others who listened to their guiding whisper, all have impacted humanity with the resultant immortal expressions of their inner voice.

As your voice on the inside grows in clarity and strength, your inspiration will grow, too as you continue to listen. Begin to become attuned to that inspiring station within. Listen as it guides you to new levels of creativity and operation. Your inner voice will put few or no limits on your life. Only the many outer voices of others who allow themselves to live a life of mediocrity will do so. Decide now to expand your wisdom and fulfillment through such careful listening. Follow the steps below and commune with this wise inner guide. It will yield through you a greater contribution to others and possibly even a legacy.

1. Stand relaxed with your hands loosely at your side.

2. Take a few deep breaths. Inhale and exhale through the nose slowly.

3. Tilt your head up 30 degrees.

4. Turn your eyes up another 30 degrees, until you are looking forward and upward.

5. Close your eyelids and let them become relaxed.

6. Think about something or someone you are truly and deeply grateful for.

7. Keep thinking and thanking until you feel your heart has truly opened up and you have even experienced a tear of inspiration.

8. Upon attaining a grateful state, now ask your inner voice for any guiding message. Ask, "Inner voice do you have a message for me at this moment?"

9. When you are grateful enough and you ask for a message, a message will clearly come.

10. Write this message down.

11. If your message does not come immediately and clearly revealed, repeat steps 6 through 10 until it does.

When you are truly grateful you will receive amazing and inspiring inner messages. These messages will be more powerful than might at first be apparent. The master, the genius, is the one who listens carefully. When you are grateful and your heart becomes opened, you will have revealed before your mind an inner message that you will have a passion to fulfill. These priceless gems of guiding revelation will assist you in living a life of greatness.

~~***~~

Chapter Eighteen:
Learn to Relax

We live in an age of tension, and there is no doubt that most of it comes from the fast pace of society and the pressure many of us feel as we try to get ahead (or just keep our heads above water). Without realizing it, most people go about their day in a state of tension that seems normal to them. They don't know what relaxation is, and they don't know that aside from making you feel nervous and anxious, it can also cause long-term problems for your health. Not only is it hard on your heart, but it also causes insomnia, high blood pressure, fatigue, depression and many other things.

Tension can hit any part of the body, but it's most common in your jaw, shoulders, neck and eyes, so it's a good idea to concentrate on them. This doesn't mean that there's no tension in other parts of your body. There is, and you should also get rid of it.

Learning to relax can help you immensely. In fact, it can change your life. You might not think of it as such, but tension is actually a habit -- a particularly bad habit. But with a little practice it can be changed into a good habit, namely relaxation. You can be relaxed and feel great throughout the day, day after day.

Think about how easy it is for a baby or small child to fall asleep. We are born with the instinct to relax and sleep when our bodies or minds need a break. Over the years, it becomes necessary to control and even suppress these natural urges to rest, since we must remain alert as we attend school, learn professions, go to work, or care for a family. Many people spend years conditioning themselves to perform well despite feelings of tiredness.

While no one would argue that suppressing tiredness could be a necessary skill, it can impair our ability to actually "let go" and relax when we do find the time.

Relaxation is also a uniquely individual activity. Napping or just doing nothing might be your idea of relaxation, but this amount of inactivity might drive someone else crazy. Others may relax by participating in sports or undertaking physical challenges, but some people would find these activities stressful. Whatever your idea of relaxation, you can regain some of those lost relaxation skills.

Tension arises primarily from the things that go on in your mind -- your thoughts. But strangely, to get rid of it, you have to concentrate on your muscles, and there are four basic techniques for relaxing them.

The techniques are:

- Deep breathing

- Direct muscle relaxation

- Music

- Visualization

Other things also help, but I will concentrate on these four.

Deep breathing is closely associated with meditation, but I'll leave the discussion of meditation to others. For deep breathing you have to begin by learning to breathe properly. Most people breathe shallowly within their chest; for "deep breathing' you have to learn to breathe from your abdomen. This means that you abdomen should be moving in and out, and not your chest. Also important is closing your mind and paying attention only to your breathing. All of us have little "conversations" going on in our mind most of the time. You can't relax if your mind is cluttered. So keep it blank and concentrate on your breathing.

A comfortable chair is also important and you should make sure your clothing is loose and comfortable. Loosen your collar and belt. Relax and think of your body as an old sock. Start by breathing smoothly, with your abdomen moving in and out; gradually deepen your breathing as you allow each breath to flow smoothly to the next. Increase it until you are breathing deeply, and then gradually decrease it. Continue doing this for 10-15 minutes.

The above can be coupled with *direct muscle relaxation*. There are two forms of this. In the first, usually referred to as *passive relaxation*, you start with the tip of your head and progressively relax each part of your body, one at a time. Think about the particular body part, and then relax it. Start with your eyes and jaw -- relax them; let them hang heavy and droop as you concentrate on your breathing. Then move down to your neck and shoulders. Continue with your arms, your mid-section, and your legs.

An alternative to direct muscle relaxation is *progressive muscle relaxation*. In this case you tense each part of the body, then release it and relax it. Again, you can start anywhere (usually with your head) and move through your body as above.

Music is also helpful in releasing tension. Again, sit in a chair and make yourself comfortable. Put some relaxing music on your stereo or iPod. It's important to find music that is relaxing to you (and this will differ significantly from person to person, depending to a large degree on your age). As you sit back, let the music wash over you, and again, focus on your breathing, and try to keep your mind clear. Just listen to the music; feel yourself relax as you listen to it. Let yourself float with the music and let it wash over you. Take an excursion into your own body and see what's there you should know about. Learning to sense our own bodies can be significant for our overall wellness and our ascension to higher consciousness. We can't deny who we are inside and expect to transcend the limitations of human existence.

Chapter Nineteen:
Help Others

While everyone is rushing around, I challenge you to stop and take a few minutes to help someone. It's fun and I guarantee that you'll feel good. It is healing to your body, mind and spirit.

"And when ye reap the harvest of your land, thou shalt not make clean riddance of the corners of thy field when thou reapest, neither shalt thou gather any gleaning of thy harvest: thou shalt leave them unto the poor, and to the stranger: I am the LORD your God." Leviticus 23:22

Weather you are Christian, Hindu, Buddhist, Muslim, or Hindu, you are somebody's life raft. Many physiological and psychological tests have been conducted regarding people who take the time to help other people (the so-called Good Samaritans), and those that don't. The results of all the studies showed that there are benefits for those that stop and help others. It has been shown to be beneficial to heart disease, neurological diseases, cancer, and a host of emotional disorders ranging from stress-related diseases to depression and anxiety.

"Give, and it shall be given unto you; good measure, pressed down, and shaken together, and running over, shall men give unto your bosom. For with the same measure that ye mete withal it shall be measured to you again." Luke 6:38

For many of my clients the act of helping others created a moment in time that shifted their attention away from themselves or their disease. This provided a haven of rest from their worries while providing a very healing and magical moment for them.

Many of us speak of Ma'at in our lives, but Ma'at cannot be attained without helping others. Creating a balanced lifestyle that includes truth, order, balance, peace, morality, happiness and service to others is Ma'at. Helping others can help you experience a lesser degree of stress as well, because as you feel more connected to your spirit, more grateful for what you have, you are less invested in the stress-producing rat race of life.

Helping others brings good feelings to both the giver and the receiver of the good deeds. Using your special gifts to help others can be a gift to yourself as you enjoy a self-esteem boost for making others' lives better, and making the world a better place. You feel more worthy of good deeds yourself, your trust in the decency of people is reinforced, and you feel more connected to yourself and to others. In fact, research shows that those who demonstrate more altruistic social interest tend to enjoy higher levels of mental and physical health above and beyond the expected. Do you have a nagging feeling that something is missing in your life? Many people find volunteering time, money, or making donations to the less fortunate makes life more meaningful. Learn more about how getting involved in a cause you believe in can help reduce stress, increase happiness, and bring more meaning to your life. These tips make it easy for people of various lifestyles.

"Help someone who can't return the favor." Author Unknown

"Do all the good you can, and make as little fuss about it as possible." Charles Dickens

"The more I help others to succeed, the more I succeed." Ray Kroc

When you are helping other people out of the goodness of your heart, beware of people who will take advantage of you. This does not mean you should not be altruistic; just beware of vampires. There are those who will try to suck the life out of you, but don't let this hinder your generosity.

"Listening is a magnetic and strange thing, a creative force. You can see that when you think how the friends that really listen to us are the ones we move toward, and we want to sit in their radius as though it did us good, like ultraviolet rays." Brenda Ueland

How well do we communicate with others? Often, when we are interacting with others, our attention in both speaking and listening is focused on meeting our own needs.

Our communication skills improve when we can be aware of the needs of the other person. When we listen, we can release the filters that serve our own needs for security and receive the message with our compassionate heart. And when we speak, we can choose words that the listener is able to receive. True communication happens when we harmonize with the other individual.

"So when you are listening to somebody, completely, attentively, then you are listening not only to the words, but also to the feeling of what is being conveyed, to the whole of it, not part of it." -- Jiddu Krishnamurti

"The first duty of love is to listen." Paul Tillich

~~***~~

Chapter Twenty:
Stop Watching Television

How many hours do you think you spend watching TV in an average week? A couple of hours? Three or four? More than twenty? If you stop to think about it, those TV hours don't take long to add up. Even in a moderate TV-watching household, it's simply amazing how many hours are spent in front of the one-eye monster. Let's see, an hour of news seven days a week, five sitcoms, a couple of movies, a quiz show, a cartoon for grownups, and a standup comedy special and the hours really add up.

Doesn't exactly sound like couch-potato material, right? But add it up - that's about sixteen hours - or two full working days' worth of time right there. And that's not even counting daytime TV or breakfast programs. Makes you think, doesn't it?

TV is a habit. If you'd like to free up more of your spare time by turning that TV off more frequently, try some of these techniques.

If you work hard all day, by the time you make it home, it's often just too hard to find the energy to do anything except flop in front of the TV and hope to be entertained while you eat dinner. If you do this five nights per week, you're in a TV rut. Chances are your sofa has grooves, which match the curves of your body. But what's the alternative? What else can you do to relax at the end of the day?

You need to become aware that it's possible to break this habit. If you have an ever-increasing pile of unread books, people to call, or after-hours work to do, it will be worth your while to reclaim at least some of your spare time and energy.

What are you eating?

Think about what you're putting into your body as you vegetate in front of the box. Are you actually nourishing your body or are you too busy watching that sitcom to even think about it? Do you routinely eat a heavy pre-packaged, fatty meal in front of the TV? If so, there's a good chance that your diet is contributing to your lethargy. Force yourself to stop off at the grocer on your way home and pick up some fresh vegetables. A stir-fry is quick and easy to make, and won't weigh you down and make you feel that it's so hard to get up again.

Just for a week, try replacing that beer with a glass or two of fruit or vegetable juice. You may be surprised when the rush of vitamins and natural sugars spark you up and make you feel that you'd rather do something more interesting than watching TV. Eating more healthily at the end of the day, and reducing your alcohol intake are also more likely to improve the quality of your sleep. A few days of this new routine, and you might find that you're not quite so exhausted when you get home.

Turn on a different appliance.

Tonight, when you get home, try this experiment. As soon as you make it in the door, pull on some comfortable clothes, and instead of reaching for the TV's remote control device, head for the stereo instead. Pop in a CD of your favorite music, preferably something uplifting and optimistic. Take some deep breaths as this wonderful sound fills your apartment. Now you're free to move around as it suits you, rather than confining your quick dashes to the bathroom to the three-minute commercial breaks.

If you're feeling unusually energetic, or you're expecting guests the following evening, try replacing the TV with another household appliance — the vacuum cleaner. A quick whiz around the carpet while dinner's cooking away on the stove and you'll have one more chore out of the way, and a great excuse to relax with a book after you've eaten.

And if the truth were told, my life didn't crash from not watching TV. Looking back, I don't feel like I have missed out on anything. In fact, I feel my life has changed for the better. In the past years of not watching TV, I have experienced numerous positive changes, such as increased consciousness, more clarity, more time to do what I want, productivity, and freedom. In fact, about a month ago, I tried watching TV again to see how it would be after so many years of not watching. I allotted myself one hour, but I couldn't last beyond 20 minutes. The shows felt boring, the programs seemed empty, and the advertisements were pointless. It just felt like a waste of time. I'd much rather be doing something else.

There are many reasons why I don't watch TV, and I'll share with you my biggest reasons why you should not watch TV either.

- **Watching TV Wastes Time**

"They put an off button on the TV for a reason. Turn it off . . . I really don't watch much TV." George W. Bush

Not watching TV has given me a lot more free time to do things I love. I remember in the past, I'd mark out shows I wanted to watch on my schedule. Then I'd arrange my activities around them. While I was watching the shows, other activities had to be put on hold. I didn't count, but I was probably spending at least 3 hours/day in front of the TV, if not more. That's quite a bit of time spent in front of the one eye-monster and doing nothing else. In retrospect, that was a big waste of my evenings.

- **TV Wastes a Lot of Time - Over Five Hours Every day**

Nielsen research showed the average American watched **an average of 5.1 hours per day**, or 153 hours of TV each month (Q1 of 2009). That's one-third of the time we are awake. This figure is increasing too, quarter by quarter. Five and one-half hrs/day is nearly 2,000 hours a year, or 78 days – **2.5 full months**. Even though these figures reflect the American population, the figures for other regions probably don't deviate much. With all this time spent watching TV, it's a wonder how we ever have time to do anything else. Just imagine if we spend a fraction of this time working on our goals– we'd already be making so much headway by now.

- **TV Gives a False Sense of Productivity**

Another thing I've noticed about TV is **how** it gives you an illusion that you're missing out from not watching. At least, it gave me that impression. The TV trailers would announce, *"This Thursday is **Blockbuster Thursday** – Be sure to catch Movie #1, Movie #2, Movie #3, back to back! You CANNOT miss this!"* Or *"This holiday season, all the best movies are coming home to you! You won't want to miss this for anything!"* For a period of time, I'd take time out to catch those shows, and then I'd feel accomplished after I'd watched them.

But these shows never stop airing. They just keep going on and on, and once you are done for the week, new trailers will run. It's like a vacuum that sucks you in and keeps you there. I also realize that I don't ever accomplish anything from watching TV. Yes, it helps me to relax and chill out at first, but after a certain amount of time I feel more sluggish and tired from watching. Then at the end of it, there's no specific output. I've gained nothing and done nothing.

- **TV Slows Down Your Brain Activity**

There's a reason why they coined the term "couch potato". Excessive TV watching turns you into a couch potato in time. Research has shown that when you are watching TV, your higher brain regions shut down, and activities shift to the lower brain regions [Source: TV: Opiate of the Masses.] Your lower brain is set in a "fight or flight" response mode. In the long run, your higher brain regions experiences atrophy due to lack of usage. There have been studies that TV viewing among children leads to lower attention span and poorer brain development.

At the end of the day, you don't need a medical study to tell you whether TV slows down your brain or not. Since TV is a one-way medium, you don't engage and interact. You only sit and watch. When I was watching TV in the past, I would feel sluggish and tired. After a while, I would feel sleepy. Compared with other activities such as talking to a friend, using the computer, reading a book, writing articles, I am a lot more active when engaged in the non-boob tube activities. Imagine spending so much time in front of TV every day; it's a matter of time before you turn into a zombie. It's not a coincidence that heavy TV watchers are also stagnant and passive people.

Here's an excerpt on the effects of TV on us:

When you watch TV, brain activity switches from the left to the right hemisphere. In fact, experiments conducted by researcher Herbert Krugman showed that while viewers are watching television, the right hemisphere is twice as active as the left, a neurological anomaly. The crossover from left to right releases a surge of the body's natural opiates-endorphins. Endorphins are structurally identical to opium and its derivatives (morphine, codeine, heroin, etc.). Activities that release endorphins (also called opioid peptides) are usually habit-forming (we rarely call them addictive).

Even casual television viewers experience opiate-withdrawal symptoms if they stop watching TV for a prolonged period of time. An article from South Africa's *Eastern Province Herald* (October 1975) described two experiments in which people from various socio-economic milieus were asked to stop watching television. In one experiment, several families volunteered to turn off their TV's for just one month. The poorest family gave in after one week, and the others suffered from depression, saying they felt as though they had "lost a friend." In the other experiment, 182 West Germans agreed to kick their television viewing habit for a year, with the added bonus of payment. None could resist the urge longer than six months, and over time all of the participants showed the symptoms of opiate-withdrawal: increased anxiety, frustration, and depression.

That's why people who watch TV have trouble quitting, because they are addicted. If we want to be conscious people living conscious lives, it's time to break out of the TV addiction.

Most TV Content Today Is Consciousness-Lowering

The average TV show today is consciousness-lowering, resonating in the levels of fear, guilt, grief, desire, and pride. This differs across TV networks of course – some channels have better content than others. My comments are in reference to mainstream channels/shows.

Here are some examples of shows that are more consciousness lowering than consciousness raising:

- *Fear Factor*, a reality TV program where people are dared into doing fearsome stunts for a sum of prize money. You see people getting scared, terrified, forcing themselves through the stunts for the prize money. The one episode I've watched required participants to eat a pie of worms, and I can say it wasn't very inspiring. I've heard about other episodes from friends, and they didn't seem to be done in good taste either.

- *Extreme Makeover*, a plastic surgery reality show that does "extreme makeovers" for participants. Participants are people who are unhappy because of their looks. They are given extreme makeovers that include surgery, after which they are shown as happy and confident. It somehow drives an underlying message to use surgery as a solution for low self-esteem.

- *Joe Millionaire*, a *Bachelor*-like show based on a ruse. Contestants compete to win the heart of a guy (Joe), thinking he is a millionaire when he's not. Throughout the show, he puts on a facade of a wealthy man living a luxurious lifestyle, which the contestants invariably believe until the show's finale when the last remaining contestant has to deal with the shocking revelation. I don't see the point behind the ruse. It seems to be more of a staged antic to draw viewers without any meaningful intent behind it.

There are several shows, however that has positive influences. For example, my wife genuinely enjoys *America's Next Top Model* (despite it's being a seemingly superficial show since it's about modeling). Tyra Banks, the show's producer, drives several empowering messages via the show. She often emphasizes on the importance of inner and outer beauty, a refreshing reminder in the image-centered world today. She also welcomes plus-sized models and shorter than average models, making a statement against the fashion industry's narrow definition of beauty as rail-thin, tall frames. I also like *The Apprentice* on the whole (despite the over-focus on finger pointing and fighting at times), due to its insights on project management and people management. The only show that I would look at apart from sports is, *Boston Med.*, a real live hospital emergency trauma room program that shows the daily workings of a metropolitan area hospital. *The Oprah Winfrey Show*, *The Ellen DeGeneres Show*, and *The Tyra Show* are empowering programs; too, based on the few episodes I've seen.

Here is one way you can determine whether something is consciousness raising. Get a sense of how you are feeling before watching the show. Then as you are watching the show, take a moment to assess how you feel.

- How are you feeling? Happy? Joyful? Upbeat? Motivated? Inspired? Or scared? Worried? Annoyed? Disgusted? Angst-Ridden? Weighed down? Stressed?

- What are you thinking? Positive thoughts or negative thoughts?

- What do you feel like doing? Do you feel motivated to take action? Make a positive difference? Or do you feel nothing? Lazy? Just want to go and sleep things away?

If it's the former group, then the content has a consciousness-raising effect; if it's the latter then you can probably do better without it.

Use the Time to Build More Meaningful Relationships

TV is one of the favorite ways in which families pass the time. They spend evenings in front of the TV screen, watching show after show. Even though everyone is sitting together in the same room, they aren't bonding with each other. Each of them is just developing an isolated connection with whatever's on the TV screen.

Now imagine if all this time were spent talking to each other. Suppose you asked about one another's day, tried to understand each other, discussed tomorrow's plans, or just hung out enjoying each other's company? Isn't that a more meaningful way to connect? Why build a connection with the television and characters on screen when you can build a connection with real people? TV might be a proxy to bond with each other, but it's clearly more fruitful to bond with real people, directly. I definitely find the latter more meaningful than the former.

Occasionally, my wife and I will look at a show together with our children. Whenever the TV is switched on, everyone gets glued to the show that's airing, and no one ever talks. Then after approximately one-two hours of television watching, the night is over and it's time to go to bed. Compare this to when we spend the two hours catching up on our day apart when we gain new levels of understanding about each other. Catching up is a lot more rewarding than watching TV together.

What's Next?

After all these years of a TV-free life, I doubt I'll ever return to watching TV regularly. With the Internet and the prevalence of social media, there's a lesser place for TV in our world today. My information and entertainment needs are readily met with the Internet and my writing. Out of my list of things I can do, TV is not even on the list.

Ray Morgan, OM.D. Ph.D.

Alternatives to TV

Here are more rewarding and fulfilling activities to replace TV:

- Exercising – jogging, swimming, playing sports, cycling, aerobics
- Hanging out with friends
- Reading a book
- Journaling, writing, drawing, painting
- Strolling / Hiking, dancing
- Taking a course in a subject of your interest
- Talking with your parents
- Organizing your room
- Meditating
- Setting your future goals
- Planning for your goals
- Doing things you love
- Working in the community with children or the elderly

~~***~~

Chapter Twenty One:
Express Yourself

Everyone has emotions – it's what makes people human. Emotions are how the body expresses what's going on inside.

Expressing feelings is natural; boredom is how a person knows it's time to try something new. Sadness is a sign of loss or pain around a difficult situation. Anger indicates a boundary needs to be set. Joy affirms the goodness of life. Enthusiasm displays passion and zest. As you stop repressing and instead start expressing your feelings, you learn to handle difficult emotions with ease.

It is known that unexpressed emotions, whether positive or negative, makes you sick. You must learn to express your feelings; you must tell your story.

I have noticed that one of the hardest things for us to do when we are communicating with someone else is to really express ourselves. How many times have you said something that just didn't come out the way you wanted it to? How many times have you said something that you really didn't mean, but you were too frustrated to stop it from being said? Learning to express one's self is really just a question of conquering the fear of making mistakes, and to make sure you know what you are talking about. A lot of people never do. Politicians usually belong in this category. But they are usually so convinced that they do know what they are talking about, that virtually everyone believes them.

Learning to listen is even harder. It has to do with trust, patience, and acceptance for others' opinions or thoughts. Even if you couldn't care less about what they say, a good listener listens anyway. What's more, some people have a fear of expressing themselves at all. They're afraid to say something that might cost them a friendship. Or they bottle everything up tight and freeze up at the mere thought of sharing their true emotions. This can be a constant struggle for people. It is, however, something that can be conquered. If you are struggling to express yourself to others, or you know of someone who struggles, then read on.

"Life is complex. Each one of us must make his own path through life. There are no self-help manuals, no formulas, and no easy answers. The right road for one is the wrong road for another. The journey of life is not paved in blacktop; it is not brightly lit, and it has no road signs. It is a rocky path through the wilderness." M. Scott Peck

We each have our own pathways to develop both personally and spiritually. They are based on our character and past experiences. No one else can identify our paths for us. Tune in to your inner guidance system and follow its direction. What every man or woman needs, regardless of their profession or the kind of work they are doing, is a vision of what their place is and may be. You need an objective and a purpose, a feeling and a belief that you have some worthwhile thing to do. What this is no one can tell you. It must be your own creation.

Many people are never taught how to deal with their emotions. Because they do not know how to deal with their emotions, they wind up repressing their emotions instead. For people who have endured painful life situations, they can wind up engaging in unhealthy behaviors to avoid dealing with their emotions, such as by abusing substances or taking out their frustrations on the wrong person. Expressing emotions is the healthiest way to release the pent up feelings.

Strategies For Dealing with Unexpressed Emotions

As you become familiar with your emotions instead of being afraid of them, it is easier to express them in the moment. Expressing your emotions may be done silently and inwardly as you experience the emotions. At other times shedding tears, punching a pillow, or laughing out loud may be the most appropriate. When a person owns their emotions, they never need to throw them at someone else or blame another for them; they just acknowledge, accept and feel them, and soon they release. Try these suggestions as a way to become comfortable expressing emotions.

Step 1.

Recognize the importance of dealing with emotions. Unexpressed emotions affect your life. For example, many people who struggle with ongoing depression or anxiety are actually angry. Because the unexpressed anger has nowhere to go, the person experiences the repressed anger as depression or anxiety. If you want to take control over your emotional life, you need to deal with your emotions instead of repressing them.

Step 2

Label your emotions. Many people who have never learned how to deal with their emotions have a difficult time even identifying what those emotions are. Some of my clients might feel anger when the emotion that they are actually dealing with is pain. Others might cry and feel sad in situations in which anger is really the more appropriate emotion. Practice labeling each emotion that you are experiencing.

Step 3

Resolve to deal with your emotions as you experience them. You must decide to deal with your emotions as you have them. Emotions must be expressed. You can either deal with your emotions as you have them, or you can put a lot of energy into repressing them or just wind up having to deal with a more powerful version of your emotions later.

Step 4

Recognize that expressed emotions do not last. If you will deal with your emotions as you have them, they will go away much faster. While you might feel incredibly angry in the moment, your anger will pass as long as you deal with it. Only repressed emotions linger for a very long time.

Step 5

Express your anger in a physical way. Anger can be daunting for many people to deal with. Anger is best dealt with physically, especially if you have a lot of repressed anger to process. Choose a physical activity that will not harm another person or yourself. Some good ways to deal with anger include punching pillows, hitting the ground with a baseball bat, popping balloons, taking a kickboxing class and going for a brisk walk.

Step 6

Cry out your pain. Tears can heal a wounded spirit, but many people have a hard time dealing with grief and sorrow. Try watching a sad movie and allowing yourself to cry for the characters. Set aside time to let yourself "wallow" for a little while. You will feel much better after a good cry.

Step 7

Comfort your fears. Many people who suffered from trauma during childhood struggle with feelings of terror. Comfort yourself through those feelings. Visualize yourself comforting the child you once were. See yourself wrapping a thick blanket around your terrified inner child and hold that child close to your heart.

Why Suppress and Repress Emotions?

Emotions are vibrations, similar to sounds. Just as a key on a piano reverberates when tapped, our body emanates a vibration when touched by experience. So why do so many of us suppress and repress emotions, even the pleasant ones? Some of us can allow sadness, anger and maybe even amusement to bubble up, but can't seem to touch the highs of joy or enthusiasm. Others can be joyful to a fault and stuff their sadness and anger down until it expresses itself in physical aches and pains. Imagine a musician playing one key or chord their whole career, not venturing into the variety of resonance among other notes. Every so often, when an old wound is triggered, a blaze of anger may blast out, scorching those nearby, or a tidal wave of sadness may threaten to drown them. It's no wonder people begin to suppress and repress emotions. Yet, it's the unexpressed emotions that are the most intimidating; they band together like bullies, waiting to pounce at a vulnerable moment. Yet when emotions are acknowledged and faced straight on, they soften, lighten and release all together.

As you stop repressing and start feeling your emotions, you will feel lighter, healthier, and more authentic as you begin expressing your feelings as they arise in an appropriate way.

~ ~***~ ~

Chapter Twenty Two:
Love Yourself

Since you are like no other being ever created since the beginning of time, you are incomparable.

~~***~~

Great forces are directing you to conform to the patterns of your society. You have DNA that has been handed down from generation to generation, coding repeated behavior patterns into your being. You have archetypal energies setting the standards for how you behave as a man or a woman, as husband or wife, as father or mother. You are immersed in consensual reality, whereby the world around you reflects societal understanding of how life has been and is to be.

At the same time, you have an even greater force within you inspiring you to wake up and recognize the reality of who you are. This force, the creative power underlying the entire universe, is urging you to create brand new standards of reality.

The status quo is blind to our creative power. Create a brand new world for yourself, one that meets your deepest needs, and you will help raise the quality of consciousness of the entire world.

"You must be the change you wish to see in the world." Mahatma Gandhi

"At the heart of personality is the need to feel a sense of being lovable without having to qualify for that acceptance." -- Dr. Paul Tournier

How do you really feel about yourself?

The most unforgiving voice of all is the one that lives inside our heads. It is the constant drone of self-criticism, less-than and not good enough that leads our memory maps, habit patterns, and fixed fantasies to the darkest of places. Silencing the *inner critic* is the first step toward rediscovering and reclaiming the authentic self.

You are perfect - mind, body and spirit. You are exactly where you need to be. You have never made a bad decision, although the consequences of your decisions may not have always turned out as you might have anticipated or expected. Sounds like a bunch of New Age nonsense, right? Well, not so much.

The factors that contribute to our evolution are myriad - nature, nurture, socialization, acculturation, collective consciousness, collective unconscious, racial memory, soul memory, in utero experience, prenatal influence - the list is seemingly endless. What often shapes us most immediately and most profoundly, however, are the instructions that we are given as we develop.

Take a few minutes to write down how you perceive yourself. Now take a look at what you wrote to see if you could identify where those characterizations about you originated. Can you pinpoint old messages from parents, teachers, and friends that led you to negative or positive conclusions about yourself? Are those messages valid today?

The beliefs we adopt as children usually don't hold much reality when we view them objectively as adults. If they are negative can you let them go? Can you begin to see yourself as a unique expression of life, a one-of-a kind genuine gift to this world? You, yourself, as much as anybody in the entire universe, deserve your love and affection. You are limitless like the ocean in your excellent qualities.

Looking for the Authentic Self

Break through what holds you back. Become more conscious of the unconscious programs that cause pain. Reduce resistance, anxiety, stress and worry. Attain new levels of self-acceptance and personal responsibility as you connect with your authentic self.

I believe that living authentically is the most important aspect of living soulfully. There is nothing more important or meaningful in life than honoring your authentic self— your true nature — and expressing it in the world. When you honor your most authentic self— your spirit — you are allowing your light to shine and touch the world. Living authentically in its simplest terms, is living your truth, the truth in your heart and soul. It's allowing yourself to be guided by divine truth and wisdom, each and every day, and doing your highest, most authentic work in the world. It's joyfully creating and living your highest purpose.

Living authentically is not always easy. It can be hard work, but the rewards are worth the effort. It requires the courage to ask yourself the hard questions and be completely honest with yourself about what is truly important to you in life and how you can live your highest good. It's following your heart's wisdom, living your truth, and being real in every sense. When you are living an authentic life, you are contributing your soulful nature and gifts to the world and thus, creating a better, more authentic and soulful life experience for us all.

How authentically are you living your life right now? Is there synergy between your inner world (your feelings, values, beliefs, needs, passions) and outer world (your relationships, job, home)?

When you live your life authentically, there is congruence between these two worlds. You close the gap between who you are, what you do, and what you want others to get about you. Others get the real you when you speak from the heart and walk your talk.

Many have discovered the liberating effects of journaling. When you journal, you are able to make sense of the thoughts in your head. Whether you are experiencing grief, anger, joy, excitement or some other kind of emotion, journaling is a liberating activity that is both confidential and effective.

Loving Yourself

Loving yourself goes above and beyond thinking you look to-die-for in that little black dress and three-inch heels. It's more than just an inner confidence and feeling comfortable in a relationship with your man or woman. It's all about being completely happy with the person that you are — the amazing traits and the flaws all in one without any qualms. Self-love is essential in having a truly fulfilling relationship with a partner. It's the basis for self-esteem and self-worth. It is not ego-based or thinking of yourself first at the expense of others. Self-love is the quintessential element in developing and maintaining a healthy sense of self. It's far easier to know your self honestly and completely when you like – and ideally love – the person that you are. If your abs aren't that flat this year, so what? You still love you for you.

Without self-love you lack the confidence of knowing that you are able to provide basic needs and desires *for yourself*. As successful a woman as you may be (as a parent, in your role at work, as a sibling, friend, or mentor), without self-love you continue to struggle with feeling worthy and emotionally independent. You rely on others for evidence of your value and self-worth, and continue to question evidence even when it is presented to you.

"Your vision will become clear only when you look into your heart." --Carl Jung

Learning to love yourself isn't easy — especially if you're a survivor of childhood abuse or neglect. But there are things you can do to boost your self-love.

- **Ask for a list of things people like about you.**

- Sometimes it can be hard to find things we like or love about ourselves. So ask other people to tell you all the things they like about you. Ask a friend, a lover, and a therapist. This isn't a replacement for your own love; it's a first step in learning to love yourself. You may need to hear the things other people like about you before you can value them in yourself.

- If hearing what people like about you is hard, ask your friends to write it down for you, or leave it on your voice mail, so you can read/listen to it over and over. Go back to it as many times as you can. Even if you don't believe that someone can like a particular thing about you, or you don't believe it exists, trust that your friend does see it and values it. When you start to hear critical voices inside your head, go back to those things your friend said/wrote about you, and remember that you are loved.

- **Make a list of the things you like about yourself.**

- Be as honest as you can. Modesty doesn't help you here; neither do old critical messages. If you're having trouble finding things you value about yourself, think about the things you value and love in your friends, then see if those things exist inside you, too. Most often, they do.

- Fill a special notebook with your list, or create a set of cards. Make the notebook as beautiful as you can; make it something that makes you feel good when you look at it. Then open it up and look at it any time you're feeling down or critical about yourself, or any time anyone says anything that triggers your criticalness of yourself.

- Look at this good-things-about-yourself book as frequently as you can. It may seem silly, but repetition really does make a difference. (Just think of the impact one critical phrase said over and over to a child by a parent can have. It really does have an effect. Now try to give that child inside you at least one truly loving phrase about yourself to hold on to.)

- **Make it part of your daily routine to praise something in yourself or think about something you like about yourself.**

- In this society, we're taught that praising ourselves is selfish and wrong. But praising ourselves for things that are good about ourselves only helps us. It is a healing thing to do and nourishes our self-worth. When we love ourselves, we're happier and more true to our own selves, and that happiness and ability to be free spreads to others.

- Go ahead. Try to think of something that you like about yourself, or something that you did today that made you or someone else feel good no matter how small it may seem. Give yourself the kind of warm praise that you would give a friend.

- **Love yourself like a friend**

- Close your eyes and think of a person you deeply love and

trust, and whom you know loves you whether friend or lover. Think about all the things you love and appreciate about them. Notice how that love feels inside you, how it makes you feel good.

- Now turn it around the other way and be your own friend, feeling that same deep love for yourself. Trust in the love, and just feel it. Let yourself see yourself through gentle eyes, with compassion and love, the way your friend does, even if you can only do it for a moment. Now let yourself receive that love, the love you have as a friend to yourself. Feel the warmth move through you. Remember how it feels, and come back to that love another time.

- **Make a note every time someone says something nice about you.**

- Every time someone tells you something about yourself that makes you feel good, write it down or make a mental note and jot it down later. When you get home, put that note in a container of "good things about me." Decorate the container however you like. Keep on adding notes, and read them over every time you need a little boost or even if you don't.

- **Have compassion for yourself.**

- If you're feeling really judgmental about something you've done or said, try to understand where the judgment is coming from. Not the immediate, surface answer, but an answer deep down inside you. Are you afraid of something, or are you feeling insecure? Do you think you did something wrong, or are you hearing the judgment of a voice from your past? Try to connect to that little kid inside of you who's feeling that way, and really listen to how he/she is feeling. Hug and reassure that kid, and let him/her know that he/she didn't do anything wrong, and that you love him/her.

- You can also think of a friend having acted as you did. Imagine how you'd feel towards them and how you'd still love them and readily forgive them. You probably wouldn't even find it bothersome. Try to feel that same love and compassion for yourself.

- **Recognize that the love has to come from you.**

- If you're a survivor of child abuse or come from a dysfunctional family, you may still be waiting for a parent to give you the love and acceptance you never got as a child. But the kind of love you need (or needed as a child) probably isn't going to come from a parent who abused you or who looked the other way while you were being abused. But it can come from you.

- It can be hard to love yourself. After all, if you didn't receive love as a child, or if some of that love was torn away from you by violence, self-hate may have built up inside you. But if you've survived this long, you have the courage and strength to love yourself and you do deserve it. So try to connect to that little child inside, that child who deserves all of your love and acceptance.

~~***~~

Chapter Twenty-Three:
Learn to Forgive

One of the thorniest and most difficult things for any of us to do is to respond to evil with kindness, and to forgive the unforgivable. We love to read stories about people who have responded to hatred with love, but when that very thing is demanded of us personally, our default seems to be anger, depression, righteous indignation, hatred, etc. Yet study after study shows that one of the keys to longevity and good health is to develop a habit of gratitude and to let go of past hurts.

Do you want to live a long, happy life? Forgive the unforgivable. It really is the healthiest and kindest thing you can do for yourself. The person that you deem your enemy may not deserve to be forgiven for all the pain, sadness, and suffering purposefully inflicted on you, but *you* deserve to be free of this potentially health-robbing evil. As Ann Landers often said, "hate is like an acid. It destroys the vessel in which it is stored."

Betrayal, aggression, or just plain insensitivity — there are a million different ways people can hurt us, and forgiveness isn't always easy. Whether you've been cut off in traffic, slighted by a family member, betrayed by a spouse, or badmouthed by a co-worker, most of us are faced with a variety of situations that we can choose to ruminate over or forgive. But forgiveness, like so many things in life, is easier said than done.

Forgiveness can be a challenge for several reasons. Sometimes forgiveness can be confused with condoning what someone has done to us. ("That's OK. Why not do it again?") Forgiveness can be difficult when the person who wronged us doesn't seem to deserve our forgiveness; it's hard to remember that forgiveness benefits the forgiver more than the one who is forgiven. Ultimately, forgiveness is especially challenging because it's hard to let go of what has happened. It is extremely important, however, to let go and forgive. Here are some reasons why:

- Forgiveness is good for your heart -- literally. One study from the *Journal of Behavioral Medicine* found forgiveness to be associated with lower heart rate and blood pressure as well as stress relief. This can bring long-term health benefits for your heart and overall health.

- A later study found forgiveness to be positively associated with five measures of health: physical symptoms, medications used, sleep quality, fatigue, and somatic complaints. It seems that the reduction in the negative effect (depressive symptoms) brought on by forgiveness, actually strengthened spirituality, aided conflict management, and relieved stress, thus positively impacting overall health.

- A third study, published in the *Personality and Social Psychology Bulletin*, found that forgiveness not only restores positive thoughts, feelings and behaviors toward the offending party (in other words, forgiveness restores the relationship to its previous positive state), but the benefits of forgiveness spill over to positive behaviors toward others outside of the relationship. Forgiveness is associated with more volunteerism, donating to charity, and other altruistic behaviors. (And the converse is true of non-forgiveness.)

So, to sum it up, forgiveness is good for your body, your relationships, and your place in the world. That's reason enough to convince virtually anyone to do the work of letting go of anger and working on forgiveness.

Alexander Pope once said, "To err is human; to forgive, divine." Believe it. You can give yourself the gift of forgiveness. Forgiveness is not something you do for someone else and it is not complicated. It is as simple as identifying the situation to be forgiven and asking yourself, "Am I willing to waste my energy further on this matter?" If the answer is "No," then that's it. All is forgiven. Forgiveness is an act of the imagination. It dares you to imagine a better future, one that is based on the blessed possibility that your hurt will not be the final word on the matter. It challenges you to give up your destructive thoughts about the situation and to believe in the possibility of a better future. It builds confidence that you can survive the pain and grow from it.

Telling the person that hurt you that you forgive him or her is a bonus, but it is not necessary for forgiveness to begin the process that heals the hurt. Forgiveness has little or nothing to do with another person because it is an internal situation.

There is nothing so bad that cannot be forgiven. Nothing!

"The weak can never forgive. Forgiveness is the attribute of the strong." Mahatma Gandhi

Forgiveness will not be possible until compassion is born in your spirit. It allows you to let go of the pain in your memory, and only when you let go of that pain will the memory cease to control you. When my memory controls me, I then become the puppet of my past.

"In this life. . . we are unable to forget whatever remains unforgiven. So, if we won't let go of some pain - whose time has now past - then who is to blame for the weight of this burden still being carried on our back?" -Guy Filey

"The only upside of anger is the person you become. Hopefully someone that wakes up one day and realizes they are not afraid of the journey. Someone that knows, that the truth is at best, a partially told story. That anger, like growth, comes in spurts and sits and in its wake leaves a new chance of acceptance and the promise of calm." (From the movie, "The Upside of Anger" starring Kevin Costner and Joan Allen)

In my practice I have counseled with those who share with me why it is wise to never forget the pain of the past, but when I look closely at their anger, sorrow, and bitterness that has hardened their faces, I also see why forgiveness is the better of the two paths. After forgiveness, comes love. You must realize that in your heart and spirit you are a beautiful person. The question then becomes, is there anything so unforgivable that should keep you connected in an emotional bondage to the person or condition that has wronged you? Standing here on the edge of enlightenment, you can choose to play small and remain where you are, or you can dive into your heart of love and experience a life more beautiful than you've ever known.

"It takes much more courage, strength of character, and inner conviction to forgive than it does to hang on to low-energy feelings." Dr. Wayne W. Dyer

My Prayer for Forgiveness

My living, loving God, I enter this moment of silence and consciously make the decision to unburden and detach myself from the painful memories of the past. I release to you everything that holds me back from my spiritual journey. I feel your power working in and through me in forgiving and letting go all that needs to be forgiven and released. Let me practice forgiveness today by starting with the little hurts within me. I will let go of all the everyday occurrences that do not go the way I want, and from this moment forward when I begin to feel any familiar feeling of anger or resentment, help me to practice your way of forgiveness by invoking your loving and peaceful presence and allowing your divine grace to surround me. And so it is.

• • •

Loving Notes:

- "One pardons to the degree that one loves." - Francois De La Rochefoucauld

- "Our capacity to make peace with another person and with the world depends very much on our capacity to make peace with ourselves." – Thich Nhat Hanh

- "Love is an act of endless forgiveness.' - Peter Ustinov

- "Genuine forgiveness is participation, reunion overcoming the powers of estrangement ... We cannot love unless we have accepted forgiveness, and the deeper our experience of forgiveness is, the greater is our love." - Paul Tillich

- "To forgive is the highest, most beautiful form of love. In return, you will receive untold peace and happiness." - Robert Muller

- "You know you have forgiven someone when he or she has harmless passage through your mind." - Rev. Karyl Huntley

- "Forgiveness is the fragrance the violet sheds on the heel that has crushed it." - Mark Twain

- "Always forgive your enemies - nothing annoys them so much." - Oscar Wilde

"And when you stand praying, forgive, if ye have ought against any: that your Father also which is in heaven may forgive you your trespasses." Mark 11:25

"Leave there thy gift before the altar, and go thy way; first be reconciled to thy brother, and then come and offer thy gift." Matthew 5:24

"Say not thou, I will recompense evil; *but* wait on the LORD, and he shall save thee." Proverbs 20:22

"Pardon, I beseech thee, the iniquity of this people, according unto the greatness of thy mercy, and as thou has forgiven this people, from Egypt even until now. And the LORD said, I have pardoned according to thy work: But *as* truly *as* I live, all the earth shall be filled with the glory of the LORD." Numbers 14:19-21

"Then came Peter to him, and said, Lord, how oft shall my brother sin against me, and I forgive him? till seven times? Jesus saith unto him, I say not unto thee, Until seven times: but, Until seventy times seven. Therefore is the kingdom of heaven likened unto a certain king, which would take account of his servants. And when he had begun to reckon, one was brought unto him, which owed him ten thousand talents. But forasmuch as he had not to pay, his lord commanded him to be sold, and his wife, and children, and all that he had, and payment to be made. The servant therefore fell down, and worshipped him, saying, Lord, have patience with me, and I will pay thee all. Then the lord of that servant was moved with compassion, and loosed him, and forgave him the debt. But the same servant went out, and found one of his fellow servants, which owed him an hundred pence: and he laid hands on him, and took him by the throat, saying, Pay me that thou owest. And his fellowservant fell down at his feet, and besought him, saying, Have patience with me, and I will pay thee all.

And he would not: but went and cast him into prison, till he should pay the debt. So when his fellowservants saw what was done, they were very sorry, and came and told unto their lord all that was done. Then his lord, after that he had called him, said unto him, O thou wicked servant, I forgave thee all that debt, because thou desiredst me: Shouldest not thou also have had compassion on thy fellowservant, even as I had pity on thee? And his lord was wroth, and delivered him to the tormentors, till he should pay all that was due unto him. So likewise shall my heavenly Father do also unto you, if ye from your hearts forgive not every one his brother their trespasses." -Matthew 18: 21-35

If you want to grow in your relationships and be healthy and happy, forgiveness is a necessity. Ego and pride are always involved in hurtful situations and, in the offended person's eyes, it would be natural to seek revenge. But unforgiveness has a way of keeping us in a constant state of chaos and trouble. Finding freedom and healing can only be achieved by resolving the unresolved issues in our lives and it must start by forgiving the person or persons who caused you pain.

Holy Prophet Muhammad (salla allahu alayhi wa sallam) said: Musa (peace be upon him), the son of Imran once asked, "Oh my Lord! Who is the most honourable of Your servants? And He replied, the person who forgives even when he is in a position of power." (Baihaqi)

We cannot expect Allah's forgiveness unless we also forgive those who do wrong to us. Forgiving each other, even forgiving one's enemies, is one of the most important Islamic teachings. Allah (SWT) says in Holy Quran: And those who shun the great sins and indecencies, and whenever they are angry they forgive. (al-Shura 42:37)

Islam teaches that God (Allah in Arabic) is 'the most forgiving', and is the original source of all forgiveness. Forgiveness often requires the repentance of those being forgiven. Depending on the type of wrong committed, forgiveness can come either directly from Allah, or from one's fellow man who received the wrong. In the case of divine forgiveness, the asking for divine forgiveness via repentance is important. In the case of human forgiveness, it is important to both forgive, and to be forgiven.

God does not forgive idol worship (if maintained until death), and He forgives lesser offenses for whomever He wills. Anyone who idolizes any idol beside God has strayed far astray. (Qur'an 4:116)

I know I'm not a perfect friend, I've broken your heart, and I've tried to mend.

Instead I made you hurt and cry, maybe I should say goodbye.

Would it be better for me to go? I asked you, and you said "No".

Why say no when I hurt you so bad, but believe me, you're not the only one that's sad.

I made my best friend hurt like mad, If I left would you be glad?

Deep in my heart, I'll always know, I'll love you always

When you forgive, you perform a miracle no one else notices.

- You do it alone- in the privacy of your inner self.

- You do it silently- no one can record your miracle on tape.

- You do it invisibly- no one can record your miracle on film.

- You do it freely- no one can ever trick you into forgiving someone.

- But when you forgive, you heal the hurt you never deserved.

Chapter Twenty-Four:
Seek the Truth Today

"Ask, and it shall be given you; seek, and ye shall find; knock, and it shall be opened unto you:

[8]For every one that asketh receiveth; and he that seeketh findeth; and to him that knocketh it shall be opened." Matthew 7:7-8

My time is limited, so I can't waste it living someone else's life. I cannot be trapped by dogma and empty-isms, which is living with the results of other people's thinking. I can't let the noise of other's opinions drown out my own inner voice. And most important, I must have the courage to follow my heart and intuition. Both my heart and intuition already know what I am set here to become. Everything else is secondary.

"What is the Truth?"

I know who you are. You may be skeptical, busy, prideful, unreachable, and angry, or maybe stressed out, fearful, or depressed; you may feel hopeless, trapped, frightened; sick, suffering, poor, weakened; or you may have had a great loss in your life such as a loved one or friend who have made their transition. Either way - there is something more to life that lies hidden that you possess the key to unlock. There is a way to be happy and have peace now, no matter what is going on in your life. There is a way out.

It has been my observation that most people don't seek the truth. They might ask someone they know what the truth is, but very seldom do they ask their Creator. And when they do, they don't follow through with **seeking** the truth. It is like the story of the Israelites in Exodus. They where willing to send Moses up the mountain to find out what God wanted of them, but they didn't want to go up the mountain themselves.

Let me explain what I mean by "seek". Imagine you are working on a hobby and you need a chisel from your workshop, so you ask your seventeen-year-old son for help in getting it for you. You know exactly where it is. You tell him where to find it — in the workshop in the top left drawer on the right side as you walk in the door. He comes back two minutes later and announces that it's not there. Exasperated, you stop what you are doing, bring him with you to the workshop and find it exactly where you told him it would be. He then says, "Oh, I didn't see it." Your son looked for the chisel. He didn't **seek** it. (I'm giving him the benefit of the doubt that he actually went to the garage.)

Now later that night you and your mate are going out to the movies. Before you leave you tell that same son that if he wants to use the extra car, you left the car key on the kitchen table. Now this time you made a mistake. You didn't leave it on the kitchen table. In fact it's not even in the kitchen. It's on the dresser in your bedroom. If your son wants to use the car, is there any doubt in your mind that he will find the key? I didn't think so. Why? Because he will **seek** it.

Just like the son seeking the keys, we need to **seek** the truth for ourselves. We can't be satisfied with someone else's truth, even if he's Moses or your father or mother. You cannot afford to be like Pontius Pilate and contemptuously ask, "What is truth?"

Sometime, somewhere you've heard someone say with conviction, "There are two kinds of truth." You might have even said it yourself. What usually follows is another sip of whatever you're drinking, and then the definitive explanation of the two kinds of truth. Something like (swallow): "there's the truth that hurts us and the truth that hurts others" or "there are truths of reason, and truths of fact" or, maybe, "there are absolute truths and then there are relative truths ..." (as Vizzini said in the *Men in Black* movie, "Wait till I get going! Where was I?") There is "the truth of the intellect and the truth of the heart," "the small truth and the great truth," and don't forget "the literal truth and the poetic truth." We've even been told of "the cold truth and the hot truth" and the "truth of names and the truth of things," but the best one I've come across goes like this: "There are two kinds of truth, the truth you can read in a book and the truth that any fool can see." Actually, if you think about it long enough, it makes no sense to say there are two kinds of truth.

True For vs. True

"There are expressions that should be avoided by those who aim to think clearly and to promote clear thinking in others. Expressions of the form, 'true for X' are prime examples. In a logically sanitized world, the following would be verboten: 'true for me,' 'true for you,' 'true for Jews,' 'true for Arabs,' 'true for the proletariat,' 'true for the bourgeoisie,' 'true for our historical epoch,' and the like. That would disallow such sentences as 'That may be true for you but it is not true for me.' The trouble with expressions like these is that they blur the distinction between truth and belief. To say that a proposition is true for S is just to say that S believes or accepts or affirms that P. This is because one cannot believe a proposition without believing it to be true. But S's believing that P, and thus S's believing that P is true, does not entail that P is true. This is obvious if anything is. There are true beliefs and false beliefs, and a person's holding a belief does not make it true. If you want to say that S believes that P, then say that. But don't say that P is true for S unless you want to give aid and comfort to alethic relativism, the false and pernicious doctrine that truth (Gr. *aletheia*) is relative." -The Maverick Philosopher

"I never give them hell. I just tell the truth and they think it's hell." Harry Truman

Playing Hide-and Seek with the Truth

When I was a child I loved to play hide-and seek. I commanded my friends or parent to count to twenty, and then ran to find a hiding place. Once in the closet, under the bed, or behind the couch, I would do my best to stifle my nervous giggles, excited to see if the person looking for me would discover where I was. At first I felt triumphant when I remained undetected, but after a while I grew restless and started to worry that the seeker had given up the game, forgotten about me, and gone on to something else. Should I come out of hiding? Should I shout out some clues? Where is he, anyway?

Like an unwelcome visitor, the truth knocks on the door of my awareness, attempting to reach me, to wake me up, to invite me out of my hiding place, to reveal new pathways and new directions for my life. I know Truth is there, but I don't answer. I panic. I hide, hoping either consciously or unconsciously that if I ignore whatever is trying to get my attention for long enough, it will go away.

Sometimes I do open the door just enough to see what's out there, but don't let whatever it is in. I close the door again and go about my business pretending the Truth isn't still standing there on my doorstep. And sometimes I get so habituated to disregarding the Truth that I even tune out the sound of its knocking, and I convince myself that it has gone away for good.

Here is something else I've learned: If as a human being I am stubborn, then Truth is more stubborn. It is also infinitely patient. It knocks again, and again, and again until I cannot ignore it anymore and am forced to get the message.

Ultimately, If don't answer I will lose this power struggle with the Truth. In the meantime, I become masterful at skills that are not in my best interest: I become an expert at avoidance, expert at evasion, expert at tuning out. This kind of expertise is one without which I would be better off, for as always, it inevitably leads to suffering.

When I play the game of avoidance I always sabotage my ability to have meaningful and truly intimate relationships. It undermines my clarity and creativity. It robs me of my capacity to be fully present in each moment. We often think we are tuning out to avoid pain, but in the end, avoidance of the Truth delivers us into the very pain, confusion, and unhappiness from which we are fleeing.

"Who is more foolish, the child afraid of the dark or the man afraid of the light?" Maurice Freehill

What is so Fearful about the Truth?

- We are afraid we will discover we have wasted time.

- We are afraid that we will have to admit we've made mistakes.

- We are afraid of what others will think when we change direction.

- We are afraid of losing what is familiar, even if it is causing us pain.

- We are afraid that once we let go of what we are holding onto, we may never find anything worth holding onto again.

- We are afraid we will look foolish, stupid, laughable, inferior, and worthless to others and to ourselves.

- We are afraid of hurting and disappointing the people we love.

- We are afraid of so many things, some we cannot even name.

~~***~~

Chapter Twenty-Five:
Develop a Personal Mission Statement

A personal mission statement introduces you to yourself, provides clarity, and gives you a sense of purpose. It defines who you are, your purpose, your mission and assignment and how to fulfill them.

WHO ARE YOU? Please tell me who you are, why you are here and what you want. If you think those are simple questions, keep in mind that most people live their entire lives without arriving at an answer.

How deeply can you answer this question? Please realize that you are the only one who can answer it. No one else can tell you who you are. You must discover this for yourself. And the challenge of knowing ourselves is no easy task. We hope this question excites rather than intimidates you. There's so much more to you than you know at present. Isn't this intriguing? Perhaps it's time to go exploring. The best way to get to know yourself is to create your own special mission statement. To do so takes time, first to know your self, then to navigate through the barrage of false emotional programming left over from childhood.

"Mysterious and intimidating to contemplate, the human brain of emotional programming is the most complex thing there is and the most difficult task it can undertake is to understand itself. I don't think God cares where we were graduated or what we did for a living. God wants to know who we are. Discovering this is the work of the soul – it is our true life's work." Bernie Siegel

Ray Morgan, OM.D. Ph.D.

Your personal mission statement will help you:

- Learn to cope with crisis and uncertainty

- Welcome changes and challenges

- Let go of old habits that don't work

- Hold on to the lesson, and let go of the experience

- Find deeper meaning and satisfaction in relationships

- Expand your horizons and your soul

- Make the impossible possible.

My Mission Statement

"My purpose for being on earth is to help others recognize, develop, and use their God-given intuitive abilities to ease suffering and grow in goodness, love, compassion, and wisdom. My mission is to help heal the ill of our generation, whether it is physical or emotional. I am on assignment to be the repairer of the breach in our ever-growing dysfunctional family system, giving wisdom, by showing how we can tap in to our wisest self and make our lives much happier and easier. My desire is to help each of us connect to the love that is eternal. That is the reason for my existence."

Your mission doesn't start in you brain; it starts in your heart.

My Motto

"Building bridges of understanding where there are breaches."

The Five-Step Plan for Creating a Personal Mission Statement

The realm of possibility exists in every cell in your body.

Most corporations in our country have corporate mission statements. The corporate mission statements are designed to provide direction, thrust, and insights among the leadership of the organization; it is an enduring statement of purpose. A mission statement acts as an invisible mentor that guides the people in the organization. It explains the organization's reason for being, and answers the question, "How are we as an organization going to accomplish our goal?" Even "The United States of America" has a mission statement called The United States Constitution. It does not matter what our leaders do in Washington DC. It must be in line with the intent of the founding fathers, the framers of the constitution.

A personal mission statement is similar to a corporate mission statement. It differs slightly but the fundamental principles are the same. A personal mission statement offers you the opportunity to establish what's important to you and gives some insights into your own vision for life. It enables you to have a clear view of your future, and by doing so chart a new course for your life, connecting you to your own unique purpose on this earth.

In his book. *The Seven Habits of Highly Effective People,* the author Steven Covey says to "begin with the end in mind." When starting to write your personal mission statement, always start with the end in mind and work backward to the present time.

A personal mission statement helps job seekers identify their core values and beliefs. Michael Goodman (in *The Potato Chip Difference: How to Apply Leading Edge Marketing Strategies to Landing the Job You Want)* states that a personal mission statement is "an articulation of what you're all about and what success looks like to you." A personal mission statement also allows job seekers to identify companies that have similar values and beliefs.

If you do not take the time to create your personal mission statement for yourself, life will create one for you and you may not like the one life creates. The biggest problem most of us have is in allowing life's circumstances to write our personal mission statement rather than writing our own. When we write our own mission statement, we are writing from our own God-given authentic soul. So, to help you get started on your personal mission statement, here are five steps to follow:

Steps toward Personal Mission Statement Development

Remember, a mission statement cannot be written in a day or even a week, it takes time to develop and for us to see and enjoy the process.

Step 1: Leave the past behind. Someone in your past might have forced you to abort your dreams and consequently you might have forgotten who you are. Your journey has molded you for your greater good, and it was exactly what it needed to be. Don't think that you've lost time. There is no shortcutting to life. It took each and every situation you have encountered to bring you to the now. And now is right on time. God never consults your past to determine your future.

Step2: Identify your past successes. Spend some time identifying four examples of personal success in recent years. These successes could be church, work, community involvement, home, etc. Write them down. If it is not on paper it doesn't exist.

a.   I developed a one-year curriculum for my church Sunday School Department.

b.   I was the leader on a team that set up a men's conference for my church organization.

c.   I helped my child's school with a fundraiser that was very successful.

d.   I developed a proposal at work that help my boss save a hundred and fifty thousand dollars in my department last year.

Step 3: Identify your core values. Develop a list of attributes that you believe identify who you are and what your priorities are. The list can be as long as you need. Once your list is complete, see if you can narrow your values to five or six most important values. Consider these points:

- What are your unique talents, gifts, and abilities?

- What are the priorities you would like to operate in? (Such values as trust, honesty, kindness, service, hard-work, friendliness, compassion, a positive attitude, industry, creativity, decisiveness, intelligence, spirituality, analytical ability, contemplative nature)

"Treat a child as he is and he will remain as he is. Treat a child as he can and should be, and he will become as he can and should be." Johann Goethe

Explore what you are all about.

Work on two things:

A. Vision: *"The end or your destination," Who you are as a person or what you can become?"*

B. Purpose: *What are your principles; those truths that you feel strongly about, that you are willing to accept as your own set of values?*

Finally, see if you can choose the one value that is most important to you.

Step 4: Identify contributions. Make a list of the ways you could make a difference. In an ideal situation, how could you contribute best to:

- The world in general – Think of an idea of how you can change the world.

- Your family – What is your contribution to your family?

- Your employer or future employers- Would your employer rehire you?

- Your friends- What kind of friend are you?

- Your community- Are giving back to your community?

- Your self- How good a self-manager are you?

Step 5: Identify goals. Spend some time thinking about your priorities in life and the goals you have for yourself.

Make a list of your personal goals, perhaps in the short-term (up to three years) and the long-term (beyond three years).

Step 6: Write mission statement. Based on the first five steps and a better understanding of yourself, begin writing your personal mission statement.

"And the LORD answered me, and said, Write the vision, and make it plain upon tables, that he may run that readeth it." -Habbakuk 2:2

Writing crystallizes thinking, distills thinking, and bridges the gap between the conscious and the unconscious.

Remember to always begin with the end in mind. You must have a picture of the end in mind.

A few years ago at one of our conferences for couples, we asked how many of the attendees were good at putting jigsaw puzzles together. Several of the people raised their hands, so I picked three people and gave them each a box with a puzzle of one thousand pieces. I told them they had three days to put the puzzle together, and the winner would receive a check for five hundred dollars. At the end of three days I called for the completed puzzle. To the surprise of the other attendees none of the puzzles were completed. I then explained to the group that I had rigged the puzzles by switching each of the box tops with the picture. The problem was each of the people trying to put the puzzles together were trying to match the picture on the box top with the puzzles inside, when someone else had the picture of the puzzle in their box. It is imperative that you have the correct picture of you in your mind and not a picture of someone else's opinion of or feelings about you. Most people are living a life of someone else.

"For as he thinketh in his heart, so is he ..." -Proverbs 23:7

Sum it up this way: "To live, to love, to learn, to leave a legacy." (First Things First: To Live, to Love, to Learn, to leave a Legacy -Stephen R. Covey)

The pilot makes a round trip trans-Atlantic flight twice a week from JFK airport in New York to London's Heathrow airport in the United Kingdom. He has been doing this for twenty-five years. When he arrives at the airport he files a flight plan with the flight dispatcher. He then gets into the cockpit and takes off. Most of the time he is two hundred miles off course because of the weather or traffic conditions. In order to land in at Heathrow, however, he must get back to his flight plan. In the same way, a personal mission statement keeps you on course for your mission.

"You never change things by fighting the existing reality, to change something, build a new model that makes the existing obsolete" -Richard Buckminster Fuller

My Final Mission Thoughts*:*

I am here to live life completely, honestly, and compassionately with a healthy dose of realism mixed in, and with the imagination and dreams that all things are possible if I set my mind to seek my truth.

About The Author

Dr. Ray (Imhotep) Morgan and his Queen, Regina (Ankhesenamen), are the founders of INSIGHT FOR THE FAMILY, INC., a community-based, marriage and family counseling service.

Dr. Ray Morgan is the clinical director of The PER ANKH Clinic of Hope Center for Integrated Health. He has also received extensive training in nutritional, herbal, and homeopathic medicine. He has helped thousands of people to discover the joy of living in divine health.

He has inspired thousands of individuals around the world who have undergone powerful health and emotional transformations in their individual lives by visiting his office and by attending his inspirational health seminars, conferences, and individual counseling sessions.

Dr. Morgan is highly sought after for lectures, conferences and speaking engagements throughout the international community. In his own unique, dynamic and entertaining style, he uplifts and motivates his audiences on a variety of health and emotional topics including detoxifications, health restoration, relationships, personal growth, and life coaching.

Dr. Morgan retired from The New York State Department of Mental Health. He holds a medical degree and two postgraduate degrees in marriage and family systems. He is a certified member of The International Homeopathic Association; a certified member of the American Association of Christian Counselors; an associate member of the American Society of Christian Therapists; and a clinical member of the International Colonic Therapists.

Dr. Morgan has lectured in Africa, Australia, Belgium, Caribbean, Egypt,

England, India, New Zealand, and throughout the United States. His extensive involvement in church and civic affairs has earned him many honors.

Together, Dr. Ray and his Queen, Regina, are blessed to be the parents of four wonderful children: Scott, Kristal, Nekia, Tobias, **two beautiful daughters-in-law Vixen and Hope;** and three grand children: Sakai, Kimari, Sanje, and Adonis.

Ray Morgan, OMD., Ph.D.
Insight For The Family, Inc.
744 St. Johns Place
Brooklyn, New York 11216
(718) 773-2196
Website:
www.InsightFortheFamily@yahoo.com

E-mail:
InsightFamily@aol.com

Other books DVDs and CDs By Dr. Ray Morgan

Book
When Two Become One
A Diamond in the Making
Published by: Author House Publishing

DVD
When Two Become One
A Diamond in the Making
Published by: Insight for the Family, Inc.

DVD
Natural Health Emporium
Making Your Body A Better Place To Live
Published by: Insight for the Family, Inc.

CD
Man of Vision and Woman of Purpose
Published by: Insight for the Family, Inc

CD
The Rites of Passage
Mentoring Boys into Manhood
Published by: Insight for the Family, Inc

CD
Before You Say "I Do"
Published by: Insight for the Family, Inc